ADELAIDE

A pocket guide to the city's best
cultural hangouts, shops, bars
and eateries

SAM TREZISE

hardie grant travel

CONTENTS

INTRODUCTION

Peter Gago, head winemaker at Penfolds, once told me, 'Adelaide is kind of like a Rolling Stones concert. Would you prefer to sit in a large theatre being elbowed in the gut every five minutes? Or would you prefer to have Mick Jagger play you an acoustic set in your living room?'

The latter is Adelaide.

This city is Australia's best-kept secret. When I'm far away, I often have to point it out on a map. When I'm closer to home, I get this feeling people think it's all a bit quiet. They couldn't be more wrong, but to be honest, we don't really care. After all, it's not a secret if everyone knows about it, right? So you, my friend, are one of the lucky ones.

Feel the joys of a city centre that's just a 30-minute commute away from crystal-clear beaches, lavish natural trails culminating in panoramic mountaintop views and opportunities to taste globally acclaimed produce, beer and wine straight from the table of the maker.

Admire the simplicity of a city centre built on a perfectly navigable grid. Here, you can park for $15 a day, get a great feed made from the freshest local ingredients for $10 and settle down to a well-balanced cocktail made from spirits distilled just around the corner without lining up or leaving your phone number for a call back. In Adelaide, quality is the decider. This city is a testament to the fact that you don't need 500 options for dinner – you realistically only need 50 good options.

Seasonally, partake in a world-class set of festivals that bring a smorgasbord of entertainment and culture. There's WOMADelaide (in March), Adelaide Fringe Festival (in February and March), and Adelaide Festival (March). If it weren't for sleep requirements, you could do something interesting 24 hours a day for two months straight.

In this book I'll give you insights into how to enjoy Adelaide, from the city centre to the suburbs and beyond. Because when you're in a town filled with Australia's secret gold, you're going to need a well-crafted treasure map.

Good luck, and take it easy.

Sam

A PERFECT ADELAIDE DAY

If you're off to an early start, the **Adelaide Central Market** is a great place to kick it off. Since you're off for a long day a silky latte from **Lucia's** and a tall cup of something freshly squeezed from **Goodies and Grains** is going to get you on track for an adventure.

Head south to Unley or Hyde Park. Sit streetside under the warm glare of a bay window in **Rosey's**, **Gingers**, **Mother's Milk** or **Pickle in the Middle** and refuel with a decorated serving of free-range eggs and smashed avocado.

If you're considering trying to nail the trifecta (wine region, walk on the beach and dinner in a laneway restaurant), I'd head south towards McLaren Vale first.

Navigate the rolling hills and vineyards of the Fleurieu Peninsula. Perch at the counter of a couple of iconic cellar doors. Quaff on a full-bodied glass of shiraz and a buttery chardonnay. For a well-rounded experience I'd suggest you try an old-world winery like **Samuel's Gorge** in McLaren Vale and a new kid on the block like **Alpha Box & Dice** in Willunga.

All these tastings are going to go to your head if you don't get some food into you. Next stop, downtown Aldinga for something baked that morning from **Home Grain Bakery**.

Head back towards Adelaide with a quick detour through Port Willunga beach for a dip in the water and a chance to feel the sand between your toes. Stay just long enough to watch the sun sink down (#sunsets) through the beams that once held up the old jetty.

Arrive back in town just before the crowds start shifting from after-work drinks into dinner mode. Get the first sitting in an East Hindley eatery. **Pink Moon Saloon** and **Gondola Gondola** are both great examples of inspired crafty cuisine coming through the South Aussie pass.

Looking for something a bit more intimate while that meal settles down? Head south through Topham Mall towards **Proof** off Waymouth, or head just a couple of doors down to **Clever Little Tailor**.

If you're leaning towards kicking it up a notch and are happy to pay for that cover charge, head west towards **Ancient World**, **Super Mild** or **Rocket** and show us those dance moves you packed in your suitcase.

ADELAIDE
OVERVIEW

REDBANKS

FREELING

NURIOOTPA
13

TANUNDA

GAWLER

PORT
GAWLER

ANGLE
VALE

LYNDOCH

WILLIAMSTOWN

ADELAIDE

SALISBURY

SEE INSET

BIRDWOOD

ADELAIDE

LOBETHAL

GLENELG

BRIDGEWATER

WOODSIDE

HAHNDORF

GULF

CLARENDON

MOUNT
BARKER

ST VINCENT

14

McLAREN
VALE

MACCLESFIELD

PORT
WILLUNGA

15

WILLUNGA

STRATHALBYN

SELLICKS
BEACH

MOUNT
COMPASS

FINNISS

YANKALILLA

GOOLWA

FLEURIEU
PENINSULA

VICTOR
HARBOR

16

CAPE
JERVIS

PENNESHAW

17

KANGAROO
ISLAND

SOUTHERN   OCEAN

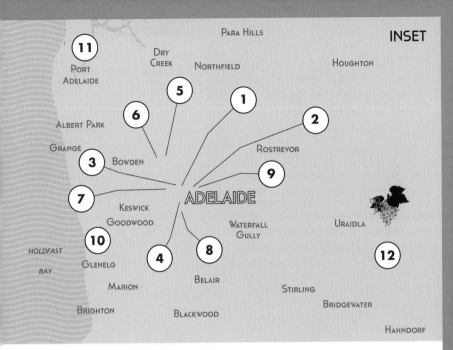

PRECINCT/

1. Central Adelaide
2. City East
3. City West
4. Market Precinct & City South
5. North Adelaide
6. Bowden, Prospect & Croydon
7. Thebarton, Mile End & Richmond
8. Inner South
9. Inner East
10. Glenelg, Brighton & Holdfast Shores
11. Semaphore & Port Adelaide

FIELD TRIP/

12. Adelaide Hills
13. Barossa Valley
14. McLaren Vale
15. Port Willunga & Sellicks
16. Victor Harbor
17. Kangaroo Island

CENTRAL ADELAIDE

Tree-lined North Terrace is home to Adelaide's major universities, the library, art galleries and museums, and a range of politically and culturally significant sites; there is no place better in the city to get access to a great set of public facilities. You can see why this boulevard replete with statues and public art was planned as a primary thoroughfare!

Adelaide Railway Station, the primary transit point to the city, sits smack bang in the middle of town. It's cuddled up to the illustrious Sky City Casino, which ironically was originally the taxation office. At Beehive Corner, legend has it that in 1954 the solid gold bee that sat atop the building's turret fell and was never recovered from an opportunistic thief. Needless to say, the replacement bee is now only gold plated.

Rundle Mall is the premier shopping stretch. In the centre sits Bert Flugelman's *Spheres* (better known as the Mall's Balls), the perfect spot to sit and watch the scene.

The historic arcades are worth a visit for their iconic charming marble floors and decorative trellising. As you exit the southern side of the arcades, the business end of Adelaide starts to take over, bringing with it busy workers who need to be fed. As a result, it's home to some super quick, easy and high-quality eats.

→ *Artwork on South Australian history in the Mortlock Wing, State Library of South Australia*

SIGHTS
1. Adelaide Arcade
2. Mortlock Wing, State Library of South Australia
3. Art Gallery of South Australia
4. South Australian Museum

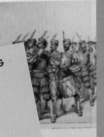

EATING & DRINKING
5. Chicken & Pig
6. Hains & Co
7. Proof / press*
8. 2KW

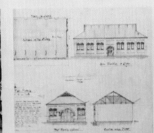

1 ADELAIDE ARCADE

Grenfell St
8223 5522
www.adelaidearcade.com.au
Open Mon–Thurs 9am–7pm,
Fri 9am–9pm, Sat 9am–5pm,
Sun 11am–5pm
[MAP 2 D3]

The arcades of Adelaide evoke a time when heading to a shopping precinct was actually a classy experience void of loud music and loitering teenagers. The marble flooring and skylit facades really help to take you back to 1855. Adelaide Arcade was the first electrically lit arcade in the world, and likely also had the first electrocuted caretaker too. They say he still haunts the corridors at night; ghost tours of the arcade can be organised at www.adelaidearcade.com.au/ghost-tours. More historical details are posted along the staircase leading to the second level near Gay's Arcade. On the first level you'll come across cobblers, tailors, watchmakers, shoe shiners, milliners and a host of other services overlooked in the 21st century. The second level of the arcade has somewhat been adopted by the cool kids. With **Boys Club Barbershop**, **Peanut Gallery** and my favourite – **Two-Bit Villains**, which serves house-made sodas and vegan diner food.

POCKET TIP
Don't miss the stall for Adelaide's **Haigh's Chocolate**, which has been providing families with delectable treats for generations.

2 MORTLOCK WING, STATE LIBRARY OF SOUTH AUSTRALIA

North Tce & Kintore Ave
8207 7250
www.slsa.sa.gov.au
Open Mon–Sun 10am–5pm
[MAP 2 D2]

You'll feel as if you've walked onto the set of a Harry Potter film in this wing of South Australia's State Library. This two-storey French Renaissance–style gem was originally set up in 1884 as the city's library, museum and gallery space, a one-stop shop for public services that now spans an entire block. Kicking back among the dimly lit marble columns and polished balustrades while flicking through one of the thousands of primary-coloured, canvas-covered hardbacks, it's easy to see why this place was ranked among the top 20 most beautiful libraries in the world. Wander downstairs and immerse yourself in a super-informative collection of displays and documents illustrating the evolution and history of all things Adelaide and South Australia. Note that the books in this library are basically decorative; if you require a functional library with a book that was written in the last hundred years, popping next door to the Spence Library might be the better option.

3 ART GALLERY OF SOUTH AUSTRALIA

North Tce
8207 7000
www.artgallery.sa.gov.au
Open Mon–Sun 10am–5pm
[MAP 2 D1]

This public gallery is housed in one of the city's most beautiful sandstone buildings, and entry is free. Inside you'll find a huge range of Australian works ranging from colonial landscapes and Indigenous sculpture to impressionist portraits and abstract installations from all around the globe. The contemporary collections and exhibitions rotate regularly, so head online to see what's on the agenda. Tours are offered at 11am and 2pm daily.

The gallery has a restaurant with a solid wine selection (what's art without wine, right?). However, if you want to keep your daytrip on the cheap side, head out the back door: the Adelaide UniBar offers basically the best-value parmi (chicken schnitzel parmigiana) and pint deal in the southern hemisphere.

4 SOUTH AUSTRALIAN MUSEUM

North Tce
8207 7500
www.samuseum.sa.gov.au
Open Mon–Sun 10am–5pm
[MAP 2 D1]

Set over five floors, the South Australian Museum aims to tell both the cultural and natural story of SA. It houses one of the largest biological collections in the world, including many coral and insect specimens, and you'll quickly see why it's such a renowned research institution. In addition to Aboriginal artefacts and minerals, meteorites and fossils from around the state, the museum displays international pieces including ancient Egyptian sarcophagi, the history of Sir Douglas Mawson's Arctic adventures and a giant squid that covers multiple levels. Free tours of the collections are offered at 11am, 2pm and 3pm. Some exhibits come with a charge, so head to the website if there is something in particular you are interested in checking out.

POCKET TIP

The Migration Museum is just around the corner. It's a great peek into the city's multicultural makeup.

5

5 CHICKEN & PIG

78 Pirie St
8227 2419
Open Mon–Fri 11am–2.30pm
[MAP 2 D3]

When you own a wood oven responsible for producing some of the most popular pizza in Adelaide (found at Pizza e Mozzarella bar, just down the street), but it only runs for half a day, what do you do the rest of the time? Chicken & Pig's solution: craft paninis and salads with the tastiest chicken and pork in central Adelaide. Besides succulent roast meat carved on the spot and pork crackling to kill for, the salad and vegetable options are something to rave about, including options like cauliflower with sour cherries and roasted celeriac. The long line might seem exhausting, but trust me, it moves fast. Be sure to get there early (before 1.30pm) or you'll likely miss your chance, because this place is only open until the roasts of the day are gone. If you're too late, Abbots and Kinney, home of all lunchtime pastries baked to perfection, is just next door.

POCKET TIP
Although some seating is offered outside, my favourite way to enjoy this food is to take it down to the grass at Hindmarsh Square and have a picnic in the sun.

6 HAINS & CO

23 Gilbert Pl
8410 7088
www.hainsco.com.au
Open Mon–Sun 4pm–2am
[MAP 2 C3]

In the laneways of Gilbert Place, Hains & Co is ornamented with seafaring relics; decorative highlights include an authentic US Navy Diving Corps helmet and a bar top recycled from an old jetty … oh, and a 1250 kilogram anchor sitting smack bang in the middle of the bar. It celebrates maritime spirits (which is pretty much all of them, but especially rum, gin and whiskey) and you'll find a hearty assortment from around the globe, and even a few from just around the corner. At the moment the food has a Southern American vibe with fried chicken, burgers and side orders of Pico de Gallo salad and chips and queso. But on a good ship the scene is ever changing, so you might see something completely different in six months.

7 PROOF / PRE*S*S*

9 Anster St / 40 Waymouth St
8212 0708 / 8211 8048
www.proof-bar.com
www.pressfoodandwine.com.au
Open Mon–Thurs 3pm–12am,
Fri 3pm–1am, Sat 4pm–1am
(Proof), Open Mon–Sat
12pm–late (press*)
[MAP 2 C3]

'Proof' might refer to the alcohol content of the huge spirit collection or proof that a Prohibition-era cocktail bar can still be unique and classy – or maybe it's a comment on the bar's strict adherence to age verification before service. Inside it's decked out with a well-executed speakeasy vibe reminiscent of the backdrop to a mid-century murder mystery; although the only crime that's going on here is that I can't afford to sample the entire menu in a night. The booze is second to none, with a diverse wine list of drops from old and new worlds. The cocktails are delicately tinkered by Shane and Joe, who are not only the licensees, but also highly regarded as pioneers in the small bar scene.

The food is served hot from the kitchen next door; press* is part of the same hospitality group and located a only a stumble away. So if Proof's bar snacks won't quite hit the spot, go for the combo with the chargrilled delights on offer at press*.

8 2KW

2 King William St
8212 5511
www.2kwbar.com.au
Open Mon–Thurs 10–12am, Fri
10–2am, Sat–Sun 12pm–12am
[MAP 2 C2]

Do you want to get high on King William Street? No, I mean, have a glass of wine on a rooftop. After you've gone through the confusing process of using two lifts and convincing two security guards that black Vans do count as dress shoes, the view from the top deck is something Instagram-worthy, with views all the way down King William Street to North Adelaide. While it comes at a cost (as platinum service often does), the menu is filled with classy stuff like mezcal and ginger sashimi, cured duck eggs in truffle oil and Wagyu rump. This sits at $65 per head; the good news is that there's also a bar menu filled with meats, cheese and pizza. In all segments of the 2KW premises, they will happily serve up their South Australian-inspired cocktail list.

CITY EAST

The city has a focus on fostering creativity in the 'State of the Arts', and nowhere is this more apparent than in the bohemian cultural precinct of the East End. The leafy, tree-lined laneways are flanked by wide sidewalks with lots of outdoor seating, the alleys are soaked in colourful work by local artists, and the area is punctuated by old sandstone archways. Filled with iconic Australian pubs, local fashion and a truly creative set of small bars by adventurous young entrepreneurs, the East End will quickly show you why locals come back time and time again.

Nestled between the busy commercial centre of Rundle Mall and the low-key parklands off East Terrace, the East End is where locals come to meet mates for brunch. Often it's not until hours later, after putting a serious dent in their wallets from shopping through the range of crafty boutiques, that they manage to leave. If time flies when you're doing what you love, then you'll hardly notice the time you spend in the East End.

EBEN

SIGHTS
1. Botanic Gardens

SHOPPING
2. Clarity Records
3. Midwest Trader
4. BNKR

EATING & DRINKING
5. The Howling Owl
6. Hey Jupiter
7. The Jade
8. Africola
9. Restaurant Blackwood
10. The Exeter
11. Botanic Bar

1 BOTANIC GARDENS

North Tce
8222 9311
www.botanicgardens.sa.gov.au
Open Mon–Fri 7.15am–5pm,
Sat–Sun 9am–5pm
[MAP 2 F1]

This is the place to go if you want to lose an entire day, come out a lot more relaxed and learn a bucket-load about Australian botany. I'd recommend grabbing some snacks and a bottle of wine from East End Cellars (an adventure in its own right) and a sandwich from East End Providore, then find a nice spot on the soft grass under a Moreton Bay fig tree. Once you've had your picnic and maybe a little nap in the sun, wander towards some of the highlights of the park, including a bamboo forest, the 1989-built Bicentennial Conservatory (the largest single-span glasshouse in the southern hemisphere) and the radiant Palm House (featuring a collection of plants from Madagascar). Oh, and don't forget the cactus park! If you're here over the summer, check out the Moonlight Cinema at the rear of the Botanic Park. As the sun sets, the silver screen goes on, and it's the best way to watch a film. Remember to pack a blanket and some insect repellent.

BOTANIC GARDENS
The Botanic Gardens stay open later during the warmer months. Closing times are extended to 5.30pm in May and August; 6pm in April and September; 6.30pm in March, October and November; and 7pm in December and January.

2 CLARITY RECORDS

60 Pulteney St
8227 1421
www.clarityrecords.net
Open Mon–Thurs 10am–6pm,
Fri 10am–9pm, Sat 10am–6pm,
Sun 12–6pm
[MAP 2 E2]

In my youth, record hunting was all about filtering through the rubbish in thrift-shop crates, dodging the scratched-up Kamahl and ABBA LPs and going home disappointed. Thankfully, these days curation is a big deal, and finding the right record store is less of a battle. The folks at Clarity are long-time supporters of the Australian (and particularly South Australian) music scene. Even if you're travelling light, take the time to speak to the owner, Footy, who is a member of the iconic punk/hardcore band Stolen Youth, then listen to some music on the turntables to learn a bit about what the scene has to offer. This place doesn't exclusively stock the fast and loud end of the spectrum – there's a gratifying range of hip hop, jazz, blues, soul, funk and everything in between. If it's time to update your suitcase or closet, nothing says edgy like a band t-shirt and a patch for your backpack; this might just be the right spot to pick up that Adelaide souvenir that you'll actually look at after you get home.

13

3 MIDWEST TRADER

1/10 Ebenezer Pl
8223 6606
Open Mon–Thurs 10am–6pm,
Fri 10am–9pm, Sat 10am–6pm,
Sun 12–5pm
[MAP 2 F2]

If you forget for a minute what continent you're on, entering this joint might make you feel like you're somewhere on America's famous Route 66. Browse the racks at Midwest Trader, where the name is misleadingly limited; the American-inspired styles here run the gamut from punk to rockabilly to hipster to cowboy, and even venture into sports. Regardless of your style, the memorabilia inside (such as a 1928 Scout motorcycle) makes it worth a look. To top it off, one of the only Australian-designed (FJ Holden) pinball machines ever produced is currently being used here as a hat rack. (I have it on good authority it still works!) If you're on the hunt for Red Wing boots, Carhartt overalls or that perfectly grungy piece of Americana, this is the spot to visit. Some of the prices are hefty; luckily, there's also a crafty selection of travel-themed patches, nostalgic rock-band pins and dapper hair greases at prices that will leave you thrilled with your great find.

POCKET TIP

If you've got the spare hours, canter around the surrounding eclectic range of retail boutiques on Ebenezer Place for the perfect mixture of well-curated, quality products.

4 BNKR

160 Rundle Mall
7009 6066
www.fashionbunker.com
Open Mon–Thurs 9am–6pm,
Fri 9am–9pm, Sat 9am–6pm,
Sun 11am–5pm
[MAP 2 E2]

BNKR is the flagship store for Australian Fashion Labels, which was born right here in Adelaide. Way before the Kardashians and Jenners got their hands on the labels, Adelaide girls had been sporting this collection of classic and eccentric boutique threads for years. The labels cover a diverse range of styles, from urban to formal. Footwear and accessories are available to complement your outfit.

In some circles, the Australian Fashion Labels collection of contemporary clothing labels is the pride of this city. Its brands, like Cameo, Finders Keepers and Keepsake, can be found in over 1800 stores worldwide, but you'd be hard pressed to find such a comprehensive range as the racks on display at BNKR. And we all know there's nothing more impressive than buying it from the source.

5 THE HOWLING OWL

10 Vaughan Pl
8227 1611
www.thehowlingowl.com.au
Open Mon–Tues 8.30am–8pm,
Wed–Thurs 8.30am–11pm, Fri
8.30–2am, Sat 12pm–2am
[MAP 2 F2]

This little sip-and-shop duo has earned a spot in the heart of many an Adelaide local. The bustling new location has doubled its capacity (more bottles of gin and gin drinkers) and there's a larger gallery space (more quirky, crafty designy delights). Howling Owl has many ginny delights on offer, representing a huge cohort of Aussie distilleries. Each and every gin is garnished uniquely with seasonal ingredients to suit the botanical structure of your spirit of choice. My order's Blind Tiger, garnished with coriander and jalapeño, packed with fresh summery flavours. As I don't condone the excessive consumption of gin on an empty stomach, you should grab yourself a grazing board filled with SA cheese and produce.

Once you're liquored up and ready to splurge, head through into Urban Cow, excelling in locally made jewellery, ceramics, quirky gift cards and screen-printed t-shirt designs. If you're lucky, there will be some locally painted artwork in the exhibition area.

6 HEY JUPITER

11 Ebenezer Pl
0416 050 721
Open Mon–Thurs 7am–5pm,
Fri 7am–7.30pm, Sat–Sun
8am–4pm
[MAP 2 F2]

Hey Jupiter offers a modern, quirky twist on a French bistro. The feature wall of antique mirrors creates a sense of spaciousness while making the place feel even more vibrantly full of people. Whether you're inside enjoying the reflections or basking in the sun in the alfresco seating, you'll be surrounded by people from all walks of life. Like a compass needle always straining north, it's hard not to be irresistibly drawn to a joint that offers crispy pork-belly sandwiches (and the cocktails for breakfast sure don't hurt). And if 'pork belly' didn't already have you drooling, other French-inspired hits on the fairly affordable menu include the breakfast cassoulet, house-made tarts and croissants, and yep, even escargot for the more adventurous patrons. If you're thirsty, have a perfectly peppered Bloody Mary … or coffee, of course. Hey Jupiter is mostly geared toward breakfast, brunch, and (late) lunches. On Friday nights, though, the friendly staff serve up great dinners.

7 THE JADE

160 Flinders St
0402 299 301
www.thejadeadl.com.au
Open Mon–Wed 8am–3pm,
Thurs–Fri 8am–late, Sat 5pm–late
[MAP 2 E4]

This historic music venue was born on Twin Street (just off Rundle Mall) over a decade ago. Tragically, that timeless haunt was replaced by a parking lot and relocated to Flinders Street. It's not all bad news, though. The new location is in the rectory of the historic Saint Paul's Church and still hosts events regularly. On sunny afternoons, the beautiful, plant-filled beer garden is the perfect place to grab some Cambodian food and a cheeky pint from the hugely comprehensive South Aussie beer list. In spring, visitors can sit in the event space lined with baby blue felt curtains and chandeliers enjoying the ever-evolving cocktail list. And in the depths of Adelaide winter, snuggle up in front of a fireplace on the cosy leather furniture after ordering a heartwarming Tasmanian whiskey. Owner Zac shares a legend about this place: a sorry bartender from generations past lost his head when playing with the dumbwaiter. Zac now keeps a mannequin head in the window upstairs so he can scare patrons after telling the story. Be sure to take a look!

POCKET TIP
Check out the graffiti in the manse room, and notice its date! Turns out there have always been pests.

8 AFRICOLA

4 East Tce
8223 3885
www.africola.com.au
Open Tues–Sat 6–9.30pm
[MAP 2 F2]

Serving up South African
cuisine in a garish yet cosy
environment, Chef Duncan
Welgemoed's Africola brings
you the delights of all things
piri piri and Boom Chakalaka.
As you sit down on the bright
blue vinyl seats with yellow
cording, noticing the food
prep all out on display, you
might be so distracted by
the activity and colour that
you forget to order – but the
exceptionally friendly staff
wearing bright harem pants
will remind you. There's a set
menu that's totally worth it if
you've got the time and money,
but it's not a requirement. The
specialty is smoky meats and
charred vegetables; I learned
quickly that 'burnt' cuisine
here is not the same as when
I cook, and in fact tastes
incredibly palatable.

9 RESTAURANT BLACKWOOD

285 Rundle St
8227 0344
www.restaurantblackwood.com
Open Tues–Fri 12–3pm (lunch),
5.30–10pm (dinner), Sat–Sun
8am–3pm & 5.30–10pm
[MAP 2 F2]

Chef Jock Zonfrillo makes a point of utilising indigenous cooking methods and focusing heavily on native ingredients. Blackwood, and its upstairs and considerably more expensive counterpart Orana, have been his outlet for this ethos. If you've never had the chance to see the way saltbush, quandong and native plum can influence cuisine (or you have no idea what any of these things are), now is your chance to give it a shot. There's a strong focus on cuts of local beef cooked over coals in the Indigenous style, and the freshly cooked Australian damper is a nice touch. The wines are very carefully chosen so as not to overpower the food, and the Vinteloper wines in particular are something different and worth a try. The candlelit vibe, high tables and polished concrete floors make for a comfortable setting. If the full, high-end experience at Orana is your cup of tea, be sure to book significantly in advance.

10 THE EXETER

246 Rundle St
8223 2623
www.theexeter.com.au
Open Mon–Sat 11–2am,
Sun 11–12am
[MAP 2 F2]

'I'll meet you at the Ex.' Not many people grow up in Adelaide without hearing that phrase regularly, and it's got nothing to do with keeping in touch with people you once dated. Unlike many modern city centres, Adelaide's downtown still has buildings that have been around since the city's formation in the 1830s. The Exeter stands out even among these antique pubs, due to her great location and unique charm. A jug of South Australia's own Coopers Pale Ale shared among good mates outside of the Exeter has been the catalyst of many a good evening. While you're here check out the grungy greenhouse-style beer garden, outdoor patio (perfect for people-watching!), fireplace-lit front-bar area and bustling band room; each offers a completely different atmosphere. Although the bar has a changing food menu throughout the week, the very affordable Curry Night on Wednesday has become an Adelaide tradition. There are gigs nightly, so be sure to ask the bar staff if something is on.

11 BOTANIC BAR

North Tce & East Tce
8227 0799
www.botanicbar.com.au
Open Tues–Thurs 5pm–12am,
Fri 4pm–2am, Sat 2pm–2am
[MAP 2 F2]

This renowned drinking hole is located in the far eastern end of North Terrace, nestled among the historic architecture and relaxing views of the Botanic Gardens and Rymill Parklands. A seat outside in the summer months in the intimate, lamplit setting calls for one of the many craft beers or boutique wines on offer. Alternatively, find your way inside, sit in a studded leather booth, perch your drink on a marble table and enjoy the atmosphere and the sounds of the low-key DJs playing in the background. Such a fine establishment calls (as they often do) for a round of cocktails. With their well-tuned knowledge of cocktails and an extensive spirits artillery at hand, the bar folk will be able to make the drink that hits the spot perfectly. If you've fallen into the trap of skipping dinner and heading straight to the bar, don't fret. The Botanic serves food from neighbouring restaurant Golden Boy, which brings to the table (literally) a perfect selection of contemporary Thai food, great for sharing among groups or satisfying the solo traveller.

CITY WEST

If you're out to indulge in all things strobe light and Jägerbomb, Hindley Street is probably your scene. But if you've outgrown that, I recommend venturing a little off this noisy thoroughfare into one of the more ambient laneway precincts.

Leigh and Peel streets have the goods when it comes to wining and dining in an al fresco-meets-laneway atmosphere. Establishments like Clever Little Tailor were the harbingers of laneway culture in this stretch, and many more have followed. Topham Mall, just south of Leigh Street, is perfect for a mid-morning wander. The creative centre of the area is around the Morphett Street Bridge. Check out the huge script-based mural of Tristan Kerr or spend some time exploring the many creative venues of the area: Arthouse cinema Mercury Cinema, design outlet JamFactory and the Lions Arts Centre are all within shouting distance. For something closer to Rundle Mall, Gresham and Bank streets have dimly lit haunts that offer you a perfect escape from the noise outside.

If you make your way to the West Terrace end of the CBD, you'll see the new site of the Royal Adelaide Hospital. The SAHMRI building next door is worth a glance too. Yes, that one, the giant cheese grater.

→ *Hindley Street artwork Mash Is Dead by Beyond Killa*

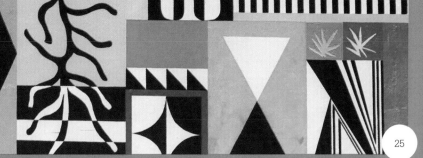

1 JAMFACTORY

19 Morphett St
8231 0005, 8410 0727
www.jamfactory.com.au
Open Mon–Sat 10am–5pm,
Sun 12–4pm
[MAP 2 A2]

This Adelaide icon just celebrated 40 years in operation. While you may expect a place called JamFactory to focus on preserved fruits, it is actually a world-renowned glass, ceramics and furniture shop. There's even a resident basket weaver! The retail space functions as a showcase for the work of local designers and residents. It's the perfect spot to get your hands on contemporary pieces, from functional kitchenware, such as pepper mills and storage jars, to collectable art pieces suiting a range of aesthetics. Exhibitions from craftsmen run regularly too, often in collaboration with the Art Gallery of South Australia and seasonal festivals like the South Australian Living Artists Festival (SALA). The site is also home to a training program, and you can actually head out to the observation deck at times and watch residents in action with glass-blowing kilns. You're encouraged to walk around the grounds and have a look upstairs to see what's going on.

2 IMPRINTS

107 Hindley St
8231 4454
www.imprints.com.au
Open Mon–Wed 9am–6pm,
Thurs–Fri 9am–9pm, Sat
9am–5pm, Sun 11am–5pm
[MAP 2 B2]

Renowned for its quality stock, Imprints bookshop is an oasis in the heart of what many consider a questionable area. And it doesn't just stock good books – it looks good, too. It's naturally lit from the large bay windows, with mahogany bookcases and a cosy couch to sit on while you flick through your finds. Since its doors opened in the '80s, Imprints has been an important piece of the West End's cultural scene. The current owners have worked there for over 20 years; their dedication to the store and the scene is apparent as soon as you walk in and ask for advice. Not only will they recommend some great reads, but they'll probably tell you about a new coffee shop around the corner too. This is one of those shops where you feel like you're a smarter and more sophisticated individual for just walking through its doors. Known for its wide range that includes philosophy, play scripts and classics, this shop is where Adelaide's well-read get their literary fix.

3 TWENTY FIFTY-TWO

83B Hindley St
7423 8153
www.twentyfiftytwo.com.au
Open Mon–Thurs 10am–6pm,
Fri 10am–8pm, Sat 10am–5pm
[MAP 2 B2]

Twenty Fifty-Two sits downstairs in a basement halfway along Hindley Street. Unlike most subterranean spaces in this area, it's filled with style. Since these guys opened their original store on Prospect Road, I've enjoyed having access to well-curated men's urban, skate and outdoor wear. The boys have a scholarly knowledge of brands and designers from both around the corner and across the globe, with a selection of footwear, outerwear, t-shirts and jeans you simply don't find anywhere else in this town. If you're seeking some of the less pervasive clothing styles and brands, this is the place to go. You'll find t-shirts, caps and outerwear from established Australian producers such as Butter Goods (Western Australia) and Pass-Port (Queensland) mixed in with a solid range of boutique offshore suppliers including Fuct, Babylon LA and LurkNYC. If all this city-hopping is wearing down your soul (and soles), pick up a fresh pair of Converse One Stars or Vans AV Classics.

4 PETER RABBIT

234-244 Hindley St
0429 098 337
www.peterrabbit.com.au
Mon–Thurs 7.30am–3.30pm,
Fri 7.30am–10pm
[MAP 2 A2]

The wacky vegetable-garden decor makes for an unusual all-day brunch spot. Organic and homey, the place looks the way its food tastes (and with some great vegetarian options, Mr McGregor is not baking too many rabbit pies in this story!). Fortunately for the real rabbits who live here, the only wolf around doesn't pose much of a threat, as he's just painted on a piano. The menu changes regularly with the seasons, much like an actual vegetable patch does. Some hearty favourites, notably the breakfast guacamole, halloumi and roast vegetables, will always be around, regardless of the shifting seasons. There are tap heads shaped like shovels and spades, which fortunately don't pour out carrot juice, so you're in luck if you're looking for a frosty pint. Hither and Yon wines are available by the glass too. If you're not up for getting tipsy, the coffee is also legitimately good; it's always a happy surprise to find that a food-focused place does its drinks this well.

5 SUNNY'S PIZZA

17 Solomon St
0408 845 993
www.sunnys.pizza
Open Wed–Sat 4pm–2am
[MAP 2 B3]

Sunny's is located on the latest of East Hindley's rejuvenated backstreets. Owned by a crew of gentlemen who have served the Adelaide hospitality scene for years, this addition to the hefty number of indulgent Adelaide pizza joints is certainly worth a visit. The decor is clever and a bit sarcastic, with some typical Little Italy vibes: ironic family pictures on the wall, pink tiled tables, and entire tins of tomatoes and bottles of Campari lining the shelves. Be sure to have a look at the signs that hang over the toilets and check out the ceramics inside (even if you don't need to go). The open kitchen, with its wood oven in the centre, pushes out some crispy Neapolitan-style pizzas with toppings including squid ink cacciatore, confit garlic and basil – and, of course, the Australian favourite, ham and pineapple. The chef certainly knows his way around a pizza oven and has cooked in a range of famous pizzerias.

POCKET TIP
On Rosina Street, check out the Matej Andraž Vogrinčič 14,910 matchbox car mural, donated by the people of Adelaide.

6 MAYBE MAE / BREAD & BONE

15 Peel St
8231 8535
www.breadandbone.com.au
Open Mon–Fri 5pm–2am,
Sat 6pm–2am, Sun 6pm–12am
(Maybe Mae), Open Mon–Sun
11.30am–late (Bread & Bone)
[MAP 2 C3]

Nestled between Hindley and Currie streets sit two streets, Leigh and Peel, that epitomise small bar and laneway culture in Adelaide. Bread & Bone is one of the top choices in the area, serving epicurean burgers and hot dogs in an off-the-wood-grill style. The Three Little Pigs (that's pork three ways: roast pork, heritage ham and smoked bacon) and the soft-shell crab burgers are my go-to, but the classic cheeseburger is timelessly satisfying.

Literally below where you just ate that burger sits the bar Maybe Mae. You'll have to look closely, because its entrance is a somewhat disguised panel in the wall. Lined with booths and mirrors, and lit by dangling green spheres, Maybe Mae serves choice cocktails, with a focus on fresh housemade juices and syrups. At times, the vibes here are that of a Manhattan lounge, but Mae has a reputation for getting a bit rowdier as midnight comes around.

7 PINK MOON ∫ALOON

21 Leigh St
0407 111 857
www.pinkmoonsaloon.com.au
Mon–Thurs 4pm–12am, Fri
12pm–2am, Sat–Sun 4pm–2am
[MAP 2 C3]

This establishment might
remind you of the old man's
house from the movie *Up*.
Wedged between two
apartment buildings, this place
is reminiscent of a Midwestern
log cabin and is a perfectly
cosy hideaway from the busy
West End streets. Pink Moon
is broken into three sections: a
front bar serving refined wines,
time-honoured cocktails and
some lesser-seen draft beers; a
central garden with seating for
casual diners and sun soakers;
and an indoor dining area if
you're looking to eat one of the
heartier meals. If you're hungry
enough, I'd recommend the
affordable behemoth of a club
sandwich, sided with hand-cut
chips. Pink Moon Deli has
recently opened for lunch too,
so if you're looking to pick up
a chicken or brisket sandwich
on the go, you've now got a
convenient central location.

POCKET TIP
Coffee Branch, up at
the end of the street, is
the perfect place to get
an espresso after you've
had a huge pastrami
sandwich for lunch.

8 CLEVER LITTLE TAILOR

19 Peel St
0407 111 857
www.cleverlittletailor.com.au
Open Mon–Sat 4–11pm
[MAP 2 C3]

Bars like CLT, which recently celebrated its fourth birthday, have played an important role in activating this precinct. Their entrance to the scene came at a pivotal time when Adelaide said, 'We've had enough – we're going to compete in this global small-bar movement!' It's hard to miss this crafty, corner East Village–looking shopfront when walking down Peel Street. It's even harder to ignore the immediate charm of the exposed stone walls and stark white weatherboard bar front. Since small bars are small by definition, you might have issues comfortably finding a seat. But if you roll in at an off-peak time, you'll have your choice of mezzanine seating either in a circular booth among pals, or against the balustrade overlooking the action below. The ever-changing draft taps and wine list makes a quick selection hard, but the team will point you in the right direction. If you're on the prowl for something a bit stronger, the whiskey selection hails from all across the map.

MARKET PRECINCT & CITY SOUTH

Victoria Square sits a short walk, and an even shorter tram ride, up King William Street from Rundle Mall. This large plot of grass, known to the Indigenous community as Tarndanyangga ('Red Kangaroo'), is the traditional meeting place of the communities in this region. The spot is still used for public events, like the Tour Down Under, Tasting Australia and the South Australia Living Artists Festival (SALA). It's also a great place to grab some street food from a food truck and have lunch on the grass. Heading northwest from the square, you'll come to the eastern entrance to the markets, with a view of the courthouses at the southern end of the square. Hop off at the tram stop here and stroll into the markets, where the stalls and food courts are filled with produce and cuisine from across the globe. The streets to the north and south of the markets (Grote and Gouger) are lined with a range of eateries, with a particular focus on Southeast and Central Asian cuisine. Crossing over to the eastern side of the square, recently launched indoor mini golf experience Holey Moley has become an unexpected and enjoyable pastime.

SIGHTS

1. Himeji Gardens

EATING & DRINKING

2. Café Troppo
3. Adelaide Central Market
4. Lucia's
5. East Taste
6. Cantina Sociale
7. Kings Head Hotel
8. La Sing Karaoke Bar

1 HIMEJI GARDENſ

South Tce
8203 7483
www.adelaideparklands.com.
au/assets/Himeji_Garden_
Brochure_web.pdf
Open Mon–Sun 8am–5.30pm
[MAP 1 E6]

Colonel William Light designed his up-and-coming utopia of Adelaide to be filled with communal parklands. To this day, the city is rich in parks; each terrace is coated in greenery. But if I could pick one park in the CBD to boast about, it would be this little fenced-off plot in the southern parklands, which, on occasion, can be relatively empty. In 1982, Adelaide received this park as a gift from its Japanese sister city Himeji, which is famous for its tremendous Edo-period castles and gardens. The influence is instantly apparent. Filled with beautiful foliage, a lovely Japanese rock garden and a lily-filled pond, this garden is the perfect place to go and get zen, relax and zone out for a while. There are sculptures and bamboo water features strewn around the garden, and if you look closely, from time to time you might see a school of baby ducklings on the waddle.

2 CAFÉ TROPPO

42 Whitmore Sq
8211 8812
www.cafetroppoadelaide.com
Open Tues–Thurs 7.30am–4pm,
Fri 7.30am–10pm, Sat 7.30am–
6pm, Sun 7.30am–4pm
[MAP 1 D5]

Café Troppo is an eco-friendly
cafe located on the historic
Whitmore Square. Its
sustainable ethos and
community vibe make it a
cherished location for locals;
its relaxing open environment,
healthy food and local produce
will make you want to sit
around for hours, and oh – the
organic and fair-trade coffee
isn't too bad either. The menu
is homespun, unpretentious
and natural. It includes
seasonal salads served
with sourdough (from $13),
homemade pizza and pot-pies
(from $6), sandwiches and
wraps (from $9.50), and you
have to try the ever-popular
kangaroo steak sandwich ($16).
If it's your first chance to taste
our national icon, I can't think
of a better way to do it. On
Friday nights they serve tapas
until 9.30pm. A great time to
head in is at the end of a busy
week on Friday, especially
when they have live music.

3 ADELAIDE CENTRAL MARKET

44-60 Gouger St
8203 7494
www.adelaidecentralmarket.
com.au
Open Tues 7am–5.30pm,
Wed–Thurs 9am–5.30pm,
Fri 7am–9pm, Sat 7am–3pm
[MAP 2 B5]

The Adelaide Central Market has been providing locals and tourists with the freshest produce from all over the country for over 140 years. You'll even catch live music and cooking demonstrations. If you wander away from the main hall, there are food courts offering every cuisine imaginable, serving breakfast, lunch and dinner for the lowest prices economically possible. Although Friday nights are popular, the freshest produce is up for grabs when the doors first open. Many of the traders here are trusted South Australian businesses that've been operating in the area for generations. **Atlas Continental** is a source of scrumptious gourmet bread, and **Cappo's Fish Market** reels in the best Spencer Gulf king prawns and Coffin Bay oysters. For your bargain fruit and veg, head to **Seven Sisters**.

4 LUCIA'S

Shop 3 Central Western Mall
8231 2303
www.lucias.com.au
Open Mon–Thurs 7am–5pm,
Fri 7am–8.30pm, Sat–Sun
7am–5pm
[MAP 2 B5]

To me, nothing encapsulates
the Adelaide markets better
than Lucia's, which is run by
a family of post-WWII Italian
immigrants who have been
bringing the goods since
the '50s. The quintessential
experience at Lucia's is as
follows: 1. Get a table in the
open seating area. 2. Organise
a tapas board filled with
succulent cured meats from
the charcuterie, then add some
fresh bread and antipasto
for good measure. 3. Order a
Negroni or glass of local wine
from inside the restaurant/
cafe. 4. Sit back and watch
the shoppers dawdle past the
market stalls as you devour
your feast.

Lucia's Pizza and Spaghetti
Bar, the southernmost of
the three Lucia's stores in
the building, also serves a
delightful range of focaccias,
pastas and pizzas. In front,
Lucia's Fine Foods gives you
an opportunity to buy some
packaged items to take away.

5 EAST TASTE

119 Gouger St
8231 0268
Open Tues–Thurs 5pm–1am,
Fri 12–3pm & 5pm–2am, Sat
5pm–2am, Sun 5pm–1am
[MAP 2 B5]

This Chinese restaurant is the foundation of late-night feasts, good times and quality food in generous proportions. Extensive menus are often questionable, but not here – every item is completely worth it. You're here for the food, not the generally kitschy decor. In fact, the past few times I've been in here, the TV was showing nothing but the Windows Vista background.

OK, let's get started with the food. Kick things off with the shallot pancakes. Try the crispy beef Peking style, the salt and pepper eggplant, the Eshand clay pot and the neighbourhood invention called BBC (for broad bean and bean curd, not the British broadcaster). This seems like a lot of food, but sharing it is always a good option to get the full experience. If you're looking for less standard fare, go for the jellyfish salad, octopus, spicy ox tripe or kangaroo.

6 CANTINA SOCIALE

108 Sturt St
8410 6246
www.cantinasociale.com.au
Open Wed 4–10pm, Thurs
4–11pm, Fri–Sat 4pm–12am,
Sun 4–10pm
[MAP 1 D5]

Tucked away from the commercial centre of Adelaide, this sheltered little bar is a gem that offers a unique experience for the wine lover. What makes it unique? All the wine comes in barrel form; wines unseen in any other venue or bottleshop are brought in, tapped and served by the glass. Uninfluenced by point systems, ratings or reputations, Cantina Sociale focuses on South Australia's premier growers, attentively selecting their wines straight from the maker.

The warm atmosphere here, somewhat reminiscent of a country barn, makes it the perfect place to settle in with friends, try a few of the rotating wines and get stuck into the seasonal tapas menu. All the nibbles are geared for wine drinking; kalamata olives, truffle-oil popcorn, and free-range chicken paté are some of the stars. The venue often brings in guest chefs for special events, tastings and more substantial meals, so be sure to check the website in advance to see if anything is on.

7 KINGS HEAD HOTEL

357 King William St
8212 6657
www.kingsheadpub.com.au
Open Mon–Sun 11–12am
[MAP 1 D5]

I've seen the good, the bad
and the ugly, and among
them all, this pub and its food
service rank very highly. The
prices are very reasonable
and the specials menu can
be an absolute steal. This is
a legitimate place to try the
iconic South Australian pie
floater, essentially a beef pie
floating in a bowl of pea soup
(trust me, it tastes better than
it sounds). If you haven't had
the chance to try a parmi
(schnitzel parmigiana) yet, the
offer of McLaren Vale chicken
or Lobethal beef for $20 is a
great deal. Wash it all down
with one of the choice pints of
ale from Prancing Pony, Rabbit
& Spaghetti or Mismatch
Brewing Company. The list
here is bountiful, with several
dedicated taps serving the
finest local drops. Sturt Street
Cellars next door stocks a
range of both veteran and new/
experimental local wines, so
be sure to pick up a bottle or
two to take back home. The
sign on the rear wall reading
'Drink better booze' is not just
for neon enjoyment, it's a rule
to live by.

8 LA SING
KARAOKE BAR

261 Gouger St
8410 2266
Open Tues–Wed 8pm–1am,
Thurs 8pm–2am, Fri–Sat
8pm–5am, Sun 8pm–2am
[MAP 1 C5]

In an unlikely location next
to a run-down deli halfway
down Gouger Street, this divey
karaoke joint is the perfect
combination of glitter and
grime. There's flashing strobes,
disco balls, neon signs and a
very public karaoke stage – no
hiding behind a private booth
in this establishment. Late at
night with friends is the way to
do this; there's an unimpressive
selection of liquor and an
impressive selection of songs.
From pop and rock tunes from
the '60s to the R&B hits of the
'90s and recent chart-toppers,
you'll have no excuse not to
blast out Natalie Imbruglia's
'Torn' or Radiohead's 'Creep'
in front of a room of people
you've never met (unless you're
from Adelaide, then you'll
know a third of them). If you
all of a sudden lose your voice,
there's always the dance floor.
And La Sing serves pad thai
and crispy spring rolls until
desperately late. Since you
might have some competition
with the karaoke regulars, I'd
suggest getting songs in early
to guarantee your moment
of fame.

NORTH ADELAIDE

This area feels very much as if it was designed for the bourgeoisie – a place for high teas, blossoming gardens and Gothic architecture – and it was, in fact designed that way, as a place for the establishment to sit up on a hill and, well, look down over the rest of the town. These days, however, this area is certainly accessible to (and enjoyed by) all.

The precinct is broken into a few key areas. The first is the O'Connell strip, which runs from the top of King William Street through the entire precinct. O'Connell offers a broad collection of reasonably priced eats, the likes of which include a famous 24-hour bakery and two of the oldest yiros (Greek-style kebab) shops in town. Melbourne Street strays off the thoroughfare, providing an assortment of homey cafes and late-night dessert bars. Crossing the River Torrens over the new footbridge brings you to the city's premier sports precinct along Memorial Drive. This area is home to the recently developed Adelaide Oval, located around the corner through Pennington Gardens from St Peter's Cathedral.

POCKET TIP
The two yiros (kebab) joints on O'Connell Street contentiously claim to be the creator of the gastronomic experience (heart attack on a plate) informally known as the AB, which is essentially a mound of hot chip with sauce, kebab meat and cheese on top.

North Adelaide's O'Connell Street

SIGHTS
1. St Peter's Cathedral
2. Adelaide Oval

EATING & DRINKING
3. Beach Bum
4. E for Ethel
5. Gin Long Canteen

1 ST PETER'S CATHEDRAL

27 King William Rd
8267 4551
www.stpeters-cathedral.org.au
Open Mon–Sat 9.30am–4pm,
Sun 12–4pm
[MAP 1 D3]

Adelaide's own little Notre Dame sits on the corner of King William Street and Pennington Terrace. Despite there being no Disney film about it, it's still worth visiting. A tour through the sandstone arches of the cathedral, which was built in 1869 in a French Gothic style, can be an interesting experience. The rose-glass windows depict stories from both South Australian history and the bible. And on my recent visit I even discovered you can own your own pipe – the organ kind – if you're willing to make a donation big enough. Be sure to come at a time when there is no service on for maximum explorability. The cathedral is staffed by welcomers during opening hours, and there are information booklets available in various languages at the back of the cathedral to allow visitors to take a self-guided tour. Free guided tours are offered on Sundays at 12.30pm and Wednesdays at 11am. Advance bookings for these tours are not required.

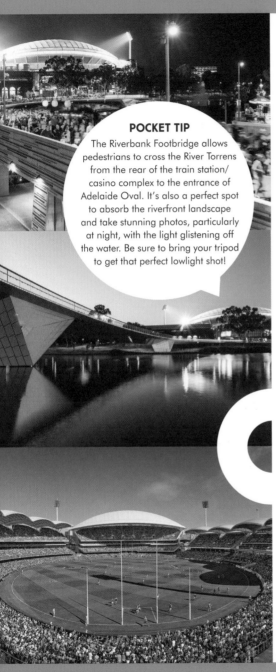

POCKET TIP

The Riverbank Footbridge allows pedestrians to cross the River Torrens from the rear of the train station/casino complex to the entrance of Adelaide Oval. It's also a perfect spot to absorb the riverfront landscape and take stunning photos, particularly at night, with the light glistening off the water. Be sure to bring your tripod to get that perfect lowlight shot!

2 ADELAIDE OVAL

War Memorial Dr
8211 1100
www.adelaideoval.com.au
Open Mon–Sun 9am–4pm
(museum)
[MAP 1 D3]

The area surrounding the Adelaide Oval has gone through huge developments lately. The introduction of the new stands and the footbridge has made this site more than just a place to watch a cricket match in the scorching summer heat. It's now home to Adelaide's AFL teams and special-event A-league (European football) games, and has even been packed out for performances from the likes of AC/DC and the Rolling Stones. Tours offer you the chance to cruise these beautiful grounds where legendary cricketer Sir Donald Bradman famously worked on his batting average as the Australians fought the English in test matches. Between the tours (which give you the opportunity to head inside the historic scoreboard) and the RoofClimb experience (where you see what it's like at the top of the stands – from the roof), you can gain some unique perspectives on the oval. The museum is currently home to the Bradman Collection and the Hill of Grace Restaurant, named for one of South Australia's most acclaimed wines.

3 BEACH BUM

47 O'Connell St
8361 8714
www.beachbum.net.au
Open Tues–Fri 11.30am–
2.30pm & 5.30–9.30pm,
Sat–Sun 5.30–9.30pm
[MAP 1 D3]

Poke (poh-KEH), a dish of seasoned raw fish with a mixture of pickled and unpickled salads drenched in sesame and soy sauce, isn't exactly considered a staple around here, and this Hawaiian/Japanese-inspired beachy joint, sporting a Kombi van as a front bar, certainly stands out in quaint north Adelaide. But this is without a doubt the best $12 lunch I've had in Adelaide for a while, with only the freshest of ingredients. It's hard to beat the choice of tuna, salmon or (cooked) chicken, especially when coupled with a glass of the house-made kombucha. It's not only the decor that comes with a hint of Japanese flavour; the menu includes a range of unique Japanese-inspired bento boxes. I wouldn't call this purely a lunch spot either; considering its solidly impressive dinner menu (including 12-hour-braised beef cheek, Hawaiian beer deals and tropically inspired cocktails), a night-time visit seems like a good idea.

4 E FOR ETHEL

116 Melbourne St
8367 0312
www.eforethel.com.au
Open Mon–Sun 9am–4pm
[MAP 1 E3]

Tucked at the back of a parking lot, E for Ethel is easy to miss. I dare say if you didn't see the sign, you'd probably not even know it was there. You'll know you're close when you come across my favourite laundromat. (Yes, I have a favourite laundromat.) The Melbourne Street Laundromat has regular gigs, free wifi and a book exchange. If you're travelling round and running low on clean clothes, the combo of this laundromat and E for Ethel might be the go! E is a stellar breakfast and lunch joint. The pancake stacks, pulled-pork soft tacos and dukkah salmon salad are all right up there, ideally washed down with one of the many available iced teas containing fresh fruit. But that's not all. E for Ethel is packed with shelves filled with quirky gifts and oddities: clay beaded necklaces, puzzles, baby clothes and some pretty darn cute gift cards. You'll leave well fed, in a fresh pair of socks, and maybe even having done some Christmas shopping.

5 GIN LONG CANTEEN

42 O'Connell St
7120 2897
www.ginlongcanteen.com.au
Open Tues–Thurs 12–2.30pm &
5.30–9.30pm, Fri 12–2.30pm
& 5.30–10.30pm,
Sat 5.30–10.30pm
[MAP 1 D3]

As you're greeted by huge mosaics of animals plastered to the wall, you can immediately tell this place is going to be interesting. Directly opposite, the kitchen runs along the entire length of the canteen. I really love sharing Asian street food, and this place does so much of it so well. It feels like there's a dish reminiscent of each Asian region. I'd suggest grabbing a few dishes and splitting them, keeping in mind that the portions are often quite generous. Highlights include the Thai classic larb gai and the slowly braised pork belly. Some bite-sized choices include the dumplings, Malaysian curry puffs and, of course, the lobster tails (if budget doesn't permit, the lobster sliders are a fitting alternative). If you're in the area at lunchtime, a specialised $12 menu is available. There's a good wine and beer list, and affordable cocktails that come in bubble tea (boba) containers; they're well balanced and tickled with flavours of lychee, tamarind and citrus.

BOWDEN, PROSPECT & CROYDON

This is the pioneering industrial area of town, with the old gasworks at its centre. You know what comes with industrial areas? Plenty of workers who need a calming ale at the end of a long day. When I lived here, I counted 11 pubs within a 10-minute walking distance. But don't worry if you're looking for something beyond a pot of draft beer, bowl of wedges and an outdated jukebox, as there are plenty of other options around. The area is dotted with a range of multicultural eateries: Afghan, Ethiopian, wood-fired pizzas and even a German bakery. It's also known as a sports and entertainment hub. Coopers Stadium, home to Adelaide United FC, sits tucked behind Port Road, and the free and direct tram makes it easy to support the mighty Reds. It's not all about scarves and jerseys either, as the precinct is also home to a thriving live-music scene. Venues like the Governor Hindmarsh play host to a range of local acts. The area is gentrifying: the old factories closer to the CBD are fading away, with apartments going up left, right and centre. Growth in the area has brought social initiatives including markets, community gardens, bicycle repair workshops and public spaces for barbecues, picnics and events.

SIGHTS & ENTERTAINMENT

1. Coopers Brewery Tour
2. Governor Hindmarsh Hotel
3. Plant 4

SHOPPING

4. Hype and Seek

EATING

5. Café Komodo
6. The Loose Caboose
7. Queen Street Café
8. Sunnys Shop

1 COOPERS BREWERY TOUR

461 South Rd, Regency Park
8440 1800
www.tours.coopers.com.au
Tours Tues–Fri 1pm
[MAP 3 C2]

As Australia's largest independently owned family brewery, Coopers Brewery is the pride of South Australian beer drinkers. These seminal SA ales are loved across Australia and the world. I have a deep personal connection to this intoxicating amber fluid, so I've been on many beer tours over the years. The one at Coopers Brewery is extremely insightful and comprehensive – I left with a good understanding of what goes into making the product and developed an appreciation for the process. For $25 per head, you'll have the chance to see the entire brewing process, taste a range of Coopers flagship brews (even some that aren't always available at the pub) and take home a tour glass. All of the proceeds of the tours go to the Coopers Brewery Foundation, which supports charities such as the Royal Flying Doctor Service. Avoid Fridays if you can, as some areas of the brewery may not be operational. Be sure to book in advance because places are limited.

2 GOVERNOR HINDMAR/H HOTEL

59 Port Rd, Hindmarsh
8340 0744
www.thegov.com.au
Open Mon–Fri 11–12am,
Sat 12pm–12am
[MAP 1 B3]

The Governor Hindmarsh ('The Gov' to close friends) has been pouring crisp pints of ale and lighting up the stage for 170 years (give or take). With a sharp focus on the alternative side of the music scene, the band room has seen some seriously famous musicians performing. But it's not just the great bands that keep people heading back – you can also share a tasty wood-oven pizza before the show, then watch the set in the leafy beer garden from a comfortable seat, with a beverage in hand that only took a few minutes to purchase and isn't spilled all over you. After (or before) the show you can swing by the charming and fully tapped front bar, which usually includes free 'entertainment' from a crowd of Irish folk singers or a crusty bunch of friendly punks. With the front bar and restaurant operating daily, and events on most nights of the week, the seamless (and free) tram trip from the city is well worth it.

3 PLANT 4

6 Park Tce, Bowden
0415 064 950
www.plant4bowden.com.au
Open Wed 4–9pm,
Sat 9am–3pm
[MAP 1 C3]

There was a time when the name 'Bowden' brought a horrifying image to my mind of contrived cool, fuelled more by the marketing plan of property developers than by local creatives. But I live there now, so you might say the marketing worked. All kidding aside, I was wrong about Bowden. Several local businesses here are doing a great job of keeping this precinct refreshingly trendy, and a real sense of community is starting to develop. The Plant 4 markets space offers up a tasty range of fresh produce, street food and local crafts. With zesty juices on tap and a bar pouring a great range of local brews, you might like to spend some time out on the grass with a glass of boutique wine. Sister Gallery on Sixth Street exhibits high-quality contemporary works from local artists, and just a stone's throw away is the Bike Kitchen, where bicycle maintenance becomes a social event. It's a great place to learn your way around the mechanics of your own bicycle.

4 HYPE AND /EEK

3 Elizabeth St, Croydon
8346 0033
www.hypeandseek.com.au
Open Wed–Sun 11am–4pm
[MAP 3 C3]

Here you'll find an
exceptionally well-curated
collection of mid-century
furniture, vintage clothing
and general crafty oddities.
If retro boutiques are your
cup of latte, this spot is a must.
In a world full of clutter and
planned obsolescence, less is
more, and everything in this
store has been hand-selected
by the owners – think Danish
telephone tables, vinyl
armchairs, Smith Corona
typewriters, black ceramic
panthers and teak lamps.
In addition to the globally
sourced vintage goods, the
owners stock a range of locally
produced items, including their
own simple modular shelving
units. The store predominately
stocks female vintage wear,
with a thoughtfully assembled
selection of summer dresses
and skirts in various patterns
and palettes that reflect the
selective and fun nature of
the store. Think less classic
cocktail dress, and more
polka dots, stripes and playful
vintage prints. It's the right
spot to visit if you want to
dress yourself (or your house)
up for a perfect vintage vibe.

5 CAFÉ KOMODO

118 Prospect Rd, Prospect
8344 7448
Open Mon–Sun 9am–4pm
[MAP 1 D1]

Keep your eyes peeled for a concealed garden passage. It leads to what appears to be the garage of a musician from the late '60s. Lamps, records and mid-century furniture fill the room. Each table is named after one of the owner's favourite musicians, and is just big enough to fit the generous servings of hearty breakfasts and vibrantly coloured coffee mugs. All-day breakfast is always something to be grateful for, but the famous Komodo plate (including dill scramble, fried tomatoes, mushrooms, sausages and bacon) might be a bit bigger than you need, so I endorse the BLAT (bacon, lettuce, avocado and tomato) for a more contained option. There are some sturdy vegetarian options, including the veggie plate or mushrooms and waffles. The venue is licensed, so you can sneak in a cheeky beer or two before heading home; something about sitting outdoors under the vines makes those beers especially tasty.

6 THE LOO*E CABOO*E

21 First St, Hindmarsh
8340 0809
www.theloosecaboose.com.au
Open Mon–Fri 7am–4pm,
Sat–Sun 8am–4pm
[MAP 1 B2]

The Loose Caboose in Hindmarsh is a quaint cafe housed in the converted Bowden railway station. Dating back to 1856, it's one of the oldest stations in the state, if not the country. Fast forward 150 years to when local couple Kate and Kim came across the derelict train station in 2015. Recognising its potential, they restored the station and opened a small cafe. They were surprised at the turnout of customers who queued up at their door in such an obscure location, but then this place is not your run-of-the-mill station coffee stand. It's charming, inventive and comfy, with hardwood floors, wooden counters, exposed brick walls and large bright windows. There's a perfect spot to sit out on the patio on a sunny afternoon too. Loose Caboose is well known for its brunch menu and house-roasted coffee brews; yours might even come served in a tiny gasoline canister. The smashed avocado on toast and hearty conductor's brunch are house staples. The servings are generous and the prices are reasonable.

POCKET TIP
Be sure to check out the mural on the side of the shop.

7 QUEEN /TREET CAFÉ

12 Elizabeth St, Croydon
0424 099 592
Open Mon–Sun 8am–4pm
[MAP 3 C3]

In this quaintly residential area, you aren't really expecting restaurants to pop up. Surprisingly, this little street (boxed in by houses in every direction) is the perfect breakfast/lunch hideaway. Some eateries come and go, but some mainstays remain, and Queen Street Café has really survived the test of time. You can sit outside on the sidewalk and the street isn't busy, so it's more pleasant than eating outside in the city. If the weather is a bit off, sit inside in one of the bay windows with a comfy cushion or two and a magazine or newspaper. They don't try to over-embellish their food here, or include too many obscure adjectives on the menu. They just do food well. Sometimes, that's all you need. My breakfast picks are the tequila and jalapeño baked eggs, and the eggs with local Harris smoked salmon. For lunch, try the chicken pesto provolone sandwich, or splurge on the crispy skin salmon.

POCKET TIP
Pick up some pastries at the nearby Red Door Bakery. I urge you to get the pork sausage roll with chilli jam, even if you need to throw it in your bag for later.

8 SUNNYS SHOP

106B Prospect Rd, Prospect
8420 0999
www.sunnysshop.com.au
Open Mon–Sat 11am–8.30pm
[MAP 1 D1]

Stamped with blue and red handpainted signage, and lined with corrugated iron and vibrant (tiny) plastic stools, this dining station is very reminiscent of meals served out of a beachside food cart on a Southeast Asian getaway. Open for lunch and serving typically Vietnamese fare, it serves tightly wrapped cold rolls, flakey bahn mi, tangy vermicelli salads and my favourite – the Asian coleslaw – which I choose to load up with Tiger Prawns and Sriracha. The dinner menu is more suggestive of the Thai end of the Southeast Asian spectrum, with portions broken down into big and small. You'll find green curries, pad thai and satay – all filled with bold and zesty flavours of lime, cashew and basil. There are plenty of vegetarian options available.

THEBARTON, MILE END & RICHMOND

This precinct is a mix of suburban and industrial zones, with some great hangouts dotted throughout. The entire region is a bit complicated to navigate on public transport, but having said that, some destinations are easy to get to, so just be sure to consult with your map before setting off. Henley Beach Road (en route to the coast) is home to the time-honoured Thebarton Theatre, which has been pulling some amazing international acts since 1927. It's a good idea to look online to see what gigs are on, because it's worth going to a performance for the venue alone. Henley Beach Road also boasts a range of lesser-seen international cuisines, including Ethiopian and Afghan, so the gig-and-feed sequence makes up a typical night out. Mile End, so named because it sits approximately 1 mile from Adelaide's town centre, is a surprising place for such a huge quantity of breakfast spots, great beer gardens and even Adelaide's only ice-skating rink. Heading further out, you can venture to Richmond, although I would advise having a destination in mind; interesting sights or spots can be few and far between if you simply go out for a stroll.

→ *A glimpse of the Adelaide Entertainment Centre*

SIGHTS
1. River Torrens Ride

SHOPPING
2. Ill-Gotten Gains

EATING & DRINKING
3. Parwana
4. Karma and Crow
5. Abyssinian
6. Chicco Palms
7. The Wheatsheaf Hotel

63

THEBARTON, MILE END &
RICHMOND

1 RIVER TORRENɼ RIDE

www.bikesa.asn.au

If you have a spare half day, one of the less well-known Adelaide activities is to head from the city to the coast on an epic bike ride down the River Torrens. Within an hour or so, you can easily pedal all the way down a clearly marked bike path, along the estuaries and parklands, to the river's mouth at Henley Beach. If you start close to Elder Park, you'll even have the chance to witness all of the new Adelaide architecture lining the precinct. After the journey, chow down on a serving of fresh fish and chips, sink your toes in the sand or enjoy a seaside pint at the **West Beach Surf Life Saving Club** before the ride back. The city offers free bike rental services, with a number of pick-up locations inside and outside the city. You can head to the Bike SA website to see a full list. There is a huge range of bike trails around South Australia, and this is one of the best spots to get started exploring them all.

2 ILL-GOTTEN GAINS

56 George St, Thebarton
0415 105 767
www.ill-gottengains.com
Open Thurs–Sun 11am–5pm
[MAP 1 B4]

For the folks behind this boutique, fashion should never be disposable; they aim to supply the market with timeless pieces. Stocking both re-creations and pre-loved vintage pieces, Ill-Gotten Gains has cornered the SA pin-up and rockabilly markets. So if hot rods and roller derby are your thing, or if you simply have a classic aesthetic, head on down. The folks at Ill-Gotten Gains will even happily make styling appointments out of hours if it suits your schedule better. Brands include Deadly Dames, Heart of Haute and many more, with wiggle dresses, cropped blouses and the like. Sizes are suitable for a range of body shapes, with everything from XS to XXL in stock. Ill-Gotten Gains is located on the same stretch as Mister Sunshine's (a great cafe brunch spot) and the Wheatsheaf Hotel (see p. 71). You will be able to make a great day trip of it, as it's only a short tram ride from the city centre.

3 PARWANA

124B Henley Beach Rd,
Torrensville
8443 9001
www.parwana.com.au
Open Tues–Thurs 6–10pm,
Fri–Sat 6–10.30pm,
Sun 6–10pm
[MAP 3 C4]

Zelmai and Farida Ayubi immigrated to Australia during the 1980s, bringing with them the authentic flavours of Afghani cuisine. Their focus was not just food, but also creating an experience filled with friendship, family, tradition and true hospitality. With the vibrant decor, collection of Afghani trinkets and sepia-tone family photos lining the walls, you feel like they have achieved what they set out to do before you even try the food. As the dishes come out, it's all 100 per cent confirmed. The rice dishes are packed with authentic flavours, as are the generous servings of gosht (tender, slow-marinated meats). There is a range of vegetarian dishes on the menu; the eggplant-based banjun borani has become a house favourite, especially when accompanied by the fluffy naan and flavoursome pickles and chutney. Most dishes fall under $20. There is no alcohol served, but corkage is available. Speak to the restaurant in advance about banquets for larger groups.

POCKET TIP
Parwana also offers great lunch specials at their second location on Ebenezer Place in the heart of the CBD.

4 KARMA AND CROW

249-251 Richmond Rd,
Richmond
8352 5104
Open Wed–Mon
7.30am–3.30pm
[MAP 3 C5]

This place is so huge that
on first arrival you may
think there's a commune
inside. Turns out the only
cult following here is for
the exceptional food and
amazing coffee. Upon strolling
through the roller door into
this hip greenhouse with its
hanging plants, you'll notice
retro furniture on polished
concrete floors. The dishes,
presented nicely and coated
in edible flowers, look so
pretty you hardly want to
disturb them. Don't miss the
orange and cardamom panna
cotta, ricotta hotcakes and
sticky roast pumpkin and feta
toast. If savoury breakfast
is what you're after, the
Korean-inspired bibimbap
is delicious.

Although this place isn't
central, and is isolated from
any useful public transport
route, visiting on the weekend
leaves you with an almost
guaranteed wait. But it's not
so bad: they serve you coffee
while you stand, and you can
always shop for records in the
pop-up huddled in the corner.

5 ABYSSINIAN

26 Henley Beach Rd,
Torrensville
8443 4300
Open Mon–Sun 5–10pm
[MAP 3 C4]

Authentic Ethiopian food is always a treat, though for some the process of an entire meal without a knife and fork is complicated. Trust me, you'll get the hang of it quickly as the spongy injera (savoury pancake) quickly becomes your plate, fork and dinner, and you enjoy the range of savoury, zesty, rich cuisine on offer. Here you can sample Ethiopian classics like tibs (sauteed meats considered a delicacy back home), gomen (braised vegetables with spices) and wot (a soupy rich stew). If you don't know your way around an Ethiopian menu, I'd suggest the Mesob experience, which will give you a balanced taste of all the hits. An extremely filling vegetarian version is available. You finish the whole thing off with a pot of hand-roasted coffee (from what many claim to be the home of this vital beverage). It's a sweeter-than-average style, but delightful all the same. The establishment is a fairly nondescript family-style restaurant, but it doesn't need to be anything else. The food speaks for itself.

6 CHICCO PALMS

437 Henley Beach Rd,
Brooklyn Park
08352 5688
www.chiccos.com.au
Open Tues–Sat 11.30am–
9.30pm, Sun 11.30am–3pm
[MAP 3 B4]

A Palm Springs–inspired Italian restaurant in the suburbs of Adelaide might seem a little farfetched, but give it a chance! If you're eating here, this is my suggested sequence of events. First, head in with multiple people, then order the giro (literally 'round' in Italian). You'll try what is essentially the entire menu. You can add pasta and antipasto to this if you want (for an extra charge), but it's already a lot of food. Then, while you wait for your food to come out of the wood oven on display, enjoy at least one aperitivo (Negroni or Aperol spritz). Finally, make sure the Stagioni pizza comes out with a glass of Tuscan rosso.

The $12 wood-fired panini here is a great option for lunch. Pick your base, cheese, then vegetables, and enjoy it with a glass of limonata. Other highlights include just about everything on the menu. Sunday roasts, spaghetti and meatballs, mac and cheese ... the meals are inspired by family favourites not typically seen on an upmarket menu.

7 THE WHEAT/HEAF HOTEL

39 George St, Thebarton
8443 4546
www.wheatsheafhotel.com.au
Open Mon–Fri 1pm–12am,
Sat 12pm–12am, Sun 12–9pm
[MAP 1 B4]

Debatably the best place to grab a pint (or several) in Adelaide, the 'Wheaty' offers up the most extensive beer list I've seen, seasonally rotating taps, and with a microbrewery out back. I'd recommend trying something local, either from the Wheaty's own selection or from Mismatch, Lobethal Bierhaus or Big Shed.

It's easy to feel as if you're in an old friend's living room at this colonial hotel full of comfortable couches, fireplaces and stained-glass windows. The laid-back characters perched at the bar or soaking up sun in the beer garden only add to the charm. Sad to say, there isn't a food menu, but it's become a tradition to have pizza from across the street delivered to the beer garden, and Uber Eats is comfortable doing drop-offs too. During busy times, food trucks conveniently set up shop by the entrance. The venue regularly has live acts, launch parties, art exhibitions and even musical swap meets, so be sure to check the calendar online for upcoming events.

INNER /OUTH

Past the grassy areas of the southern parklands lie several arterial boulevards perfect for escaping the CBD for an afternoon. These areas are mostly simple to access by public transport and lie within 15 minutes of Adelaide's city centre. To the east on Goodwood Road, you'll find the showgrounds. Here's where anxious students go to complete their exams, and where families go to enjoy the Royal Adelaide Show each September. There's a farmers' market here on Sundays. Further east sits the neighbourhood of Unley. This is the perfect place for a fancy brunch on a Sunday, with a bunch of places to choose from. Even further east lies Glen Osmond and Parkside, home to a range of cuisines and eateries. You can take this route out of the city up to the freeway towards Melbourne and the east coast. My favourite place on this stretch is Latin American restaurant Hispanic Mechanic in Frewville.

ENTERTAINMENT
1. Capri Theatre

SHOPPING
2. Flourish Gift and Home
3. Carto Graphics

EATING & DRINKING
4. Pickle in the Middle
5. 50sixone
6. Earl of Leicester
7. Nook Nosh

1 CAPRI THEATRE

141 Goodwood Rd, Goodwood
8272 1177
www.capri.org.au
[MAP 1 C7]

If you've ever wanted to know what it was like to attend a cinema 80 years ago, the Capri Theatre is probably your best shot. Originally called the Star Theatre, this heritage-listed Art Deco building is a real marvel to hang out in and the perfect place to enjoy a night of nostalgia. The cinema still plays the classics several nights a week, but if you don't actually want to sit through two hours of Charlie Chaplin, new releases are regularly on offer too. The traditional Wurlitzer organ (one of the few that remain in Australia) rises up from the ground and still accompanies the films on special occasions. The candy bar sells all the original treats, helping to create an authentic old-time experience for all of your senses.

2 FLOURISH GIFT AND HOME

114 King William Rd, Hyde Park
8373 1129
www.flourishgiftandhome.com.au
Open Mon–Wed 10.30am–
5.30pm, Thurs 10am–8pm,
Fri 10.30am–5.30pm,
Sat 9.30am–5pm,
Sun 11am–5.30pm
[MAP 1 D7]

You never know what you'll
be walking out with when
you visit Flourish. My last
trip I popped in to pick up
a couple of things to spruce
up the living room; a hand-
woven throw rug, some
scented candles – you know,
the kind of stuff to convince
your loved ones you're an
adult. But I walked out with
an Australian-designed rain
jacket, Myrtle and Moss hand
cream, a Creole cookbook that
fuelled my desire to give the
kitchen another go, and a cast
resin Elk necklace, made in
Australia, that passed the test
with my girlfriend. Flourish's
second store can be found on
Magill Road, if you happen to
be in the area.

3 CARTO GRAPHIC/

147 Unley Rd, Unley
8357 1777
www.cartographics.com.au
Open Mon–Fri 9.30am–5pm,
Sat 10am–4pm
[MAP 1 E7]

In a book full of hip coffee
shops, cocktail lounges and
shopping boutiques you
might not have expected me
to include a map store. But
let's be honest here: maps and
guides are the bee's knees,
right? If you're heading out
of Adelaide on that outback
adventure you best prepare
well – get your trail guides,
hiking companions and GPS
data locked down long before
you're stuck in the desert.
Heck, these guys will even
sell you a guide to bushcraft
and outback cooking. If
you're planning on heading
overseas to your next port of
call, these guys offer guides,
companions, phrasebooks and
power converters for every
conceivable plan you've got,
not to mention a nifty bunch
of travel accessories that will
help you on your way.

4 PICKLE IN THE MIDDLE

134 Unley Rd, Unley
8172 1083
www.pickleinthemiddle.com.au
Open Mon–Sun 8am–4pm
[MAP 1 E7]

Trust me, I don't just head here for the swanky Scandinavian furniture, slick trendy atmosphere and pickle-filled modular shelving units. The food is so good that I'd be a happy man if I could have breakfast here every day of the year. Pickle in the Middle was originally located in the Central Market (*see* p. 38), selling their now famous toasted sandwiches (with pickles and cheese in the middle). Due to incredible popular demand, they decided to open up a storefront on Unley Road. Although they still make their own preserves, the food has risen to a higher level than the original toasted sandwiches, and all the food, including the bread and conserves, is produced in-house. If you're looking for something a bit fancier, the poached egg sardines or black sesame waffles are house favourites. Although the coffees are entirely on point, if you're keen to wash it all down with something a bit different, the turmeric tonics and kombucha are quite the treat.

5 50∫IXONE

144A King William Rd,
Hyde Park
8271 2003
www.50sixone.com
Open Mon–Sun 7am–11pm
[MAP 1 D7]

After walking through the courtyard you step into something that looks like Willy Wonka meets Iron Chef. But you may have to wait – this place gathers a huge queue on weekends, because the desserts are just as huge. They're oversized not just in volume but also in flavour, in what the place calls an 'assault to the senses'. The famous shakes come in Mason jars filled with vibrantly coloured creamy goodness topped with thick syrups and coated in anything from Oreos to fairy floss. The sheer number of things they manage to cram onto, into and around your dessert must be the result of some kind of wizardry. The price tag on these bad boys might be a bit more than one would regularly expect ($20 plus), but you're paying for an experience, not just a thickshake. There is an equally impressive number of plated options, including waffles and velvet pancakes. Despite being a dessert bar, it's open from 7am, so there is a great collection of savoury diner-style breakfast and lunch options too.

6 EARL OF LEICE∫TER

85 Leicester St, Parkside
8271 5700
www.earl.com.au
Open Mon–Sat 9–12am,
Sun 10am–10pm
[MAP 1 E7]

There's a private club at the
Earl of Leicester: the infamous
beer legends list. You join by
completing the well-curated
set of 82 beers. You'll get your
name on the wall, a T-shirt and
endless bragging rights. Beers
on offer range from a humble
pint of Heineken to a decadent
Barossa Valley Coffee Stout.
My favourite spot to sit in the
Earl is at the front bar among
the stained-glass windows,
raised polished wood tables
and raw stone balustrades.
Take a seat and try one of the
monumental herb-crumbed
beef or chicken schnitzels.
The rest of the menu is a
mixture of pub classics and
modern Australian cuisine.
Weekly highlights include
50-cent wings on Tuesdays
and an incredibly hearty
Sunday roast. Quizmasters (a
lot more exciting than your
average quiz night) runs every
Wednesday. Although TVs in
pubs are generally a red flag,
these guys offer a comfortable
spot for people to watch the
game outside the house.

7 NOOK NOƧH

111 Unley Rd, Unley
7325 0313
www.nooknosh.com.au
Open Wed–Thurs
4–10.30pm, Fri 4pm–12am,
Sun 4–8.30pm
[MAP 1 E7]

Sometimes you want to escape the city without travelling too far, and Nook makes a perfect hidey-hole, as it's just a simple bus or Uber trip away. The owner is passionate about promoting the lesser-known South Australian wines. In fact, the only thing that's not South Aussie is the Champagne. Nook Nosh boasts brands like Gestalt, Matriarch & Rogue, Artwine, Shut the Gate and Grand Casino. The beer menu is just as interesting, stocking bottles from across the state.

The foods are designed for sharing, and the flatbreads topped with fresh ingredients are a good option. If you're keen for something extra on the side, the grilled halloumi or duck terrine will certainly serve that purpose. With continually rotating art on display and live music on Friday nights, Nook Nosh has an artsy feel.

INNER EAST

Growing up, I thought of this area as the Beverley Hills of Adelaide, although you might be disappointed if you head there with this in mind. All the same, something about the leafy green lanes, the upmarket clientele, the European cars lining the streets and the abundant skinny mochas gives it that ritzy air. Streets like the Parade and Magill Road are filled with shopping boutiques, upmarket patisseries and potentially my favourite supermarket in Adelaide, Foodland on the Parade, which stocks Mediterranean fare that's overlooked by other areas. This place also seems to have become a mecca for burger joints and faux Route 66–style ice-cream shops and diners. I mean, seriously … four burger places in 400 metres? The other eastern areas, including Magill, Kent Town and Dulwich, are scattered with some great little hang-outs hidden among the residential streets and small-scale office complexes. A 15-minute bus ride from the city centre, this area makes for a quick and easy getaway.

→ Norwood Parade, the primary thoroughfare in the area

SIGHTS
1. Z Ward
2. Little Bang

SHOPPING
3. Big Star
4. A Trip to the Moon

EATING & DRINKING
5. Nordburger
6. Magill Estate

1 Z WARD

25 Conyngham St, Glenside
8223 1234
www.zward.com.au
[MAP 1 G6]

Tours of this former asylum offer a ghastly insight into the checkered past of Adelaide's mental health system. This particular block of Glenside Hospital was reserved specifically for those inmates who were criminally insane, and I can unequivocally say that being locked in a cell at midnight in Z Ward was one of the most terrifying things I've ever done. Luckily I knew – unlike many who had entered before – that I was getting out in 10 minutes. Z Ward offers both night-time and daytime experiences, and its website will direct you to both. Night tours are conducted by Haunted Horizons, which also offers a double pass that includes a trip to the historic Adelaide Gaol (a similarly terrifying location). Creepy stories aside, the building itself, completed in 1885, is fascinating. To this day, this site is full of compelling architecture, high ceilings and stunning window decor across multiple levels. Tour availability can be limited, so be sure to research in advance. Pricing starts at around $38 per head and varies depending on times and package deals.

2 LITTLE BANG

8A Union St, Stepney
0417 085 692
www.littlebang.com.au
Open Fri–Sat 12–9pm,
Sun 12–5pm
[MAP 1 G3]

There's nothing quite like walking into a brewery and ordering a beer that's just been kegged a few metres away, then having a chat with the man who made it, getting him to fill up a 2-litre jug of it and taking it back home with you. The people at Little Bang have been trying to get these miraculous brews out to the world for a while now – but it's tough when 80 per cent of their 22-deep brew list gets drunk almost directly from the tank. My recent tasting session consisted of the Pinkening Hibiscus Sour, the American Sleazy Ale, and the Galactopus (10 per cent ABV), which is so alcoholic it's technically considered Australia's only barley wine. If you want to make a day of it, check out the Eastern Beer and Wine trail, which includes tastings at several inner metro wineries as well as Little Bang. If you can't make it out to this place, limited stock is available at the Kings Head (*see* p. 42), Low & Slow (*see* p. 100) and the Wheatsheaf Hotel (*see* p. 71).

3 BIG ✶TAR

160 Magill Rd, Norwood
08 8362 8393
Open Mon–Wed
10am–5.30pm,
Thurs 10am–9pm,
Fri 10am–5.30pm,
Sat–Sun 10am–5pm
[MAP 1 G4]

My mother used to head to the mall across the road and come back to this record store an hour later to find me still flicking through the crates, dust building up on my fingertips. I still get that warm feeling when I'm inside – there's nothing quite like listening to old aficionados debating the relative importance levels of Miles Davis albums. The walls are lined with old longboxes and sun-faded posters, the owner wears a West End trucker cap and I'm thrilled to report that the store is actually filled with people. Selling recently pressed and used vinyl, this joint's got a really nice selection (and there are still heaps of CDs available too). The store's genres of focus include punk, hip hop, jazz, blues and soul, and they have an impressive amount of Aussie vinyl.

4 A TRIP TO THE MOON

155 The Parade, Norwood
7225 5673
www.atriptothemoon.com.au
Open Mon–Fri 9.30am–
5.30pm, Sat 9.30am–5pm,
Sun 11am–5pm
[MAP 1 G4]

I'm a big fan of shops that you don't really need to walk into with a specific purpose, stores that are just a collection of things the owner thinks are worth selling, showing off or owning. A Trip to the Moon has just such a collection of cool homewares. There's something irresistible about looking through the assortments of cushions, lighting and quirky decorations, including a huge range of Marimekko aprons, placemats and napkins. In addition, there's a great selection of arts and crafts supplies, candles, incense and gift ideas for adults and kids. Cool travel supplies always catch my eye, and the assortment here is great. Options include travel wallets, backpacks, drink bottles and the Crumpled Maps series of waterproof maps. You'll be sure to walk out with something that catches your eye.

5 NORDBURGER

168 The Parade, Norwood
8331 9923
www.nordburger.com
Open Mon 10.30am–9pm,
Tues–Wed 10.30am–9.30pm,
Thurs 10.30am–10pm,
Fri–Sat 10.30am–10.30pm,
Sun 10.30am–10pm
[MAP 1 G4]

Keep your eyes peeled for Nordburger's emerald green flags; they're beacons of saturated, fried, cheese-drenched hope in a world of shoddy burger bars. The owners of the Botanic, Africola and Golden Boy were quick on the uptake with the burger trend and have kept up their reputation for years now. Keep it simple with the Nord's cheesy, bacony classics. If you're looking for something that's a 'burger with the lot', try the Big Kahuna, a solid choice with either beef or chicken. The Parm is a pretty iconic SA flavour too. Try tater tots or crinkle-cut chips with fry sauce on the side – and if you're really keen to get down and dirty, get them loaded. Wash the food down with your choice of iconic US pop, or milkshakes made from the Rainbow Island custardy soft serve. Surprisingly, peanut butter and jelly is the milkshake flavour of choice around here.

6 MAGILL E/TATE

78 Penfold Rd, Magill
8301 5551
www.magillestaterestaurant.com
Open Wed–Thurs 6.30–11pm,
Fri–Sat 12–3pm & 6.30–11pm
[OFF MAP 1 G4]

Magill Estate is home to the world-renowned Grange Hermitage (Bin 95), Max Schubert's iconic shiraz. This is often regarded as the wine responsible for consolidating the position of Australian wines on the global stage. The newly renovated cellar door is located on the historic estate grounds, and the estate offers tours and tastings daily. You can partake in the Heritage Tour ($20) or the Ultimate Penfolds Experience ($150), which includes a tasting and a more in-depth explanation of the grounds. Tour bookings are essential, so be sure to call ahead.

As is often the case, good food and good wine go hand in hand, and there is no better place to experience precision pairing than at the Magill Estate Restaurant. Each dish has been crafted to accompany a member of the flagship Penfolds range. If the price tag is too much for your budget, don't fret! The recently renovated Magill Estate Kitchen is a quality alternative offering both a la carte dishes and a set-menu option for breakfast and lunch.

GLENELG, BRIGHTON & HOLDFAST SHORES

Take a short trip on the tram from the middle of the city, and it's all palm trees, grassy knolls and crisp lagers on painted barstools by the ocean. This is where the original settlers first landed to carry their entire lives to the settlement in the CBD. We now commemorate this journey each year by doing the city to bay fun run. Just kidding – but it sure is a tough jog!

From the sparkly marinas lined with million-dollar yachts at Holdfast Shores to the homey family-owned eateries that have fed Adelaidians for generations, there's sure to be something for everyone. This area is also home to the Beachouse, an entertainment complex once known as Magic Mountain. With mini golf, dodgem cars and more, it's the most fun a kid can have in Adelaide. This entire stretch of beach, which lies on the eastern coast of the Gulf St Vincent, is home to some fascinating sea life, including sea horses, squid and a huge range of fish. This particular coastline plays an important role in the region's ecological system, which you can learn more about at the Bay Discovery Centre in Moseley Square.

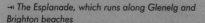

→ *The Esplanade, which runs along Glenelg and Brighton beaches*

GLENELG, BRIGHTON &
HOLDFAST SHORES

1 JETTY TO JETTY WALK

If the sun's out and the
weather's right, chances are
you're not the only person
who's showed up at the beach.
If you're thinking to yourself,
'Of the thousands of miles of
coastline, why is everyone in
this 50-metre radius?', I've
got an alternative for you: the
7.6-kilometre walk between
Henley Square (Henley
Beach) and **Moseley Square**
(Glenelg). Starting the walk
from either of these locations is
equally pleasant. You'll be sure
to find a completely isolated
spot to sit, relax and enjoy the
beautiful coastline without
the crowds. The terrain is
completely flat and waterside,
perfect for dogs and children.
There's a selection of cafes,
pubs and eateries at each
end, so you'll have a chance
to sit down and relax before
returning; all up the return
walk should take three and a
half hours including significant
breaks. Aim to be back close
to sundown, so you have the
chance to experience the
beautiful sunset; you can check
the times for this kind of thing
online beforehand. Nothing
says Instagram appreciation
like a full-spectrum sunset.

2 C.R.E.A.M

4/49 Jetty Rd
8298 3149
Open Mon–Sun 7am–4pm
[MAP 3 B7]

What an unexpected
location for an East Coast
hip-hop-themed bar. Its
name is a playful twist on the
Wu-Tang Clan's album title
C.R.E.A.M – but in this case
it stands for Coffee (rather
than Cash) Rules Everything
Around Me. Over the kitchen
pass are the words 'Bring the
Rukkas' (I can only assume
they mean food and not gang
violence) and over the exit it
says 'protect ya neck' (which
I'm hoping refers to wearing
sunscreen). Although the
walls are lined with graffiti
and hip-hop insignia, and the
staff sport fitted caps and are
coated in tattoos, the scene
is still surprisingly intimate,
with an unexpected chic-mod
kind of charm. The milk is
steamed in a gold-plated
frothing pitcher, and the
Five Senses coffee is some
of the best in Adelaide. For
breakfast, it's worth heading
there for the bowls alone. The
cubanos/sandwiches are a
very reasonably priced lunch,
and I'd particularly recommend
the Ol Dirty B*stard
fried-chicken sandwich.

3 BEACH BURRITO

56 Jetty Rd, Glenelg
8376 3772
www.beachburritocompany.com
Open Mon–Thurs 11am–
9.30pm, Fri–Sun 11am–11pm
[MAP 3 B6]

Born in Sydney's Bondi, this
little franchise has popped up in
a few places around Australia.
At the Jetty Road edition you'll
find wide-open dining upstairs
and downstairs, where you
can watch the beachy folk
strolling past with towels and
thongs. The mural on the wall
outside reads 'Glenelg, a place
to relax' – and rightly so, as
kicking it off with a couple of
margaritas or a Dos Equis is a
pretty good option. The words
'franchise' and 'Mexican food'
in the same sentence might
conjure the idea of something
bland or generic, but I promise
you that at this place, this
couldn't be further from the
truth. The ingredients are
fresh and the burritos (whether
in bowl, fajita or traditional
form) are tasty options. I go
for the slow-roasted shredded
beef with pickled vegetables
and black beans. The tacos
and quesadillas are a brilliant
alternative, with inventive
ingredients like chickpeas,
halloumi and tofu.

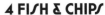

4 FISH & CHIPS

In South Australia, the fish component of fish and chips is often as fresh as it can get: pulled straight out of the Indian Ocean. We go beyond your typical deep-fried mullet and freezer-burned crinkle-cut chips. Wrapped in paper, carried under your arm to the perfect location ... it's all part of the experience. Many places will also serve an entire basket of seafood, including prawns, scallops and calamari. I head to the perfectly located **Brighton Jetty Café** when I'm along this stretch. The batter is crispy, the chips are always piping hot and the servings are huge. Glenelg is usually a bit busier, so I enjoy sitting in the bar at **The Moseley**, which has the perfect seaside view but less of the beachfront bustle. You know what goes well with beer-battered chips here? Yep. Beer. At **West Beach Chicken and Seafood**, get the Ocean Basket. There's a lovely tabled area just down the street on the beachfront with a park bench to sit at adjacent to the Surf Life Saving Club. In Henley Beach at the **Stunned Mullet**, the crumbed King George whiting is the best in town. In addition, these guys have a huge range of battered delights to choose from.

ƒEMAPHORE & PORT ADELAIDE

With their warehouses and marine support industries, port towns always seem to offer a glimpse back in time. Historic sandstone pubs, mosaic facades, maritime architecture and gold-leaf signage complete the picture. But it's not all old news in Port Adelaide. Historic Hart's Mill is now the home to the touring Saint Jerome's Laneway Festival each summer, where alternative acts from around the world come to turn it up to 11. Semaphore, just a bridge away, takes you from river to ocean, where it's all sand between your toes, seagulls and coastal air. The area is home to several age-old fish and chip stores, but Soto's Fish Shop (in operation for over 60 years) is always my first 'port of call' when it comes to paper-wrapped decadence. Stock yourself up with a delicious paper sack of deep-fried goodness and set yourself up down the street to watch the area's style unfold before you (but watch out for the seagulls, they've been known to take small children.) Before you plan your day in Semaphore, check the schedule at the Workers Club pub. It's not exactly a secret society, but it is something very special, with cheap drinks, great meals and good live music ranging from folk to gypsy jazz. You don't have to be a Leninist to enjoy walking through this iron wall (well, it's more like a tin gate).

→ *Artwork by iconic Adelaide artist KAB 101 on an old flour factory.*

SIGHTS
1. Maritime Museum
2. Fishermen's Wharf Market

EATING
3. Low & Slow
4. Drummer Boy Cafe

1 MARITIME MUSEUM

26 Lipson St, Port Adelaide
8207 6255
maritime.history.sa.gov.au
Open Mon–Sun 10am–5pm
[MAP 3 B1]

We're a country 'girt by sea', as our national anthem puts it, so it's no surprise that, historically, most immigrants and the industries that supported them were brought by nautical vessels. It turns out these boats are incredibly well documented – so much so that the Maritime Museum has a searchable database that will show you the path someone with your surname might have taken to get here. On top of this, they have a replica of a type of boat called a ketch, and a huge range of maritime artefacts including maps, telescopes, replica models and more, so you can learn a little about what life would have been like for immigrants as they voyaged across the pond in the 1870s. If boats haven't given you that transportation museum fix, the South Australian Aviation Museum, featuring an F111 Hornet, is located just around the corner. And if boats and planes aren't enough, the National Railway Museum is not too far from that.

2 FISHERMEN'S WHARF MARKET

Port Adelaide
8341 2040
www.fishermenswharfmarkets.com.au
Open Sun–Mon 9am–5pm
[MAP 3 B1]

Don't let the name deceive you – I don't actually think any fish is sold at the impressive Fishermen's Wharf Market, or any produce at all for that matter. In fact, it's two storeys of bric-a-brac, trinkets, book collections, vintage toys and clothing. This 2-storey complex will have you walking around for hours, feeling like you're the host of an episode of *Hoarders* in a space the size of an airplane hangar. From bobbleheads of South Australian sporting stars to Australian flags embedded in collectable spoons, this might be a great place to pick up a souvenir or two. Haggling is not exactly commonplace, but some vendors are clearly having a laugh, so feel free to try. The heritage-listed Port Adelaide Lighthouse stands tall just outside the entrance to the market. Built in 1869, this old boy ensured the safe passage of ships entering the river. These days, you're welcome to head up top from 10am to 2pm on weekdays and 10am to 4pm on weekends.

99

3 LOW & SLOW

17 Commercial Rd,
Port Adelaide
0402 589 722
www.lowandslowamerican
bbq.com
Open Wed–Thurs & Sat 6–9pm,
Fri & Sun 12–2.30pm & 6–9pm
[MAP 3 B1]

What happens when Australian chefs do a barbecue voyage across America? Hickory smoked, 16-hour-braised plates of delicious goodness, that's what! For $35 per head, you can have the entire works: all of the daily barbecue offerings and three glorious sides. I had the dry-rubbed brisket, pulled pork, and hot wings, supported by apple slaw, incredibly creamy mac and cheese, and tater tots that I dipped in a zesty blue-cheese relish. The window seating makes for the perfect spot for looking out over the lighthouse square. The staff are super friendly and passionate, and man do they know their barbecue. If you ask nicely, they might even let you have a look at the cooker in action. And what's a plate of slow-cooked animal without a refreshing ale? A solid range of US and South Aussie beers are on offer. If you're stickin' with the southern theme, go for the Founders IPA or the Golden Road. If you're going local, hit something from Little Bang (*see* p. 85).

4 DRUMMER BOY CAFE

132 St Vincent St, Port Adelaide
www.drummerboy.com.au
Open Mon–Fri 7am–3pm,
Sun 9am–2pm
[MAP 3 A1]

A few years ago, the idea of sipping an espresso in a cafe of this calibre in this area was just a dream; mum-and-dad snack bars and corner delis were the extent of the options. But that's all changed. Serving up coffee to the beat of a different drum, Drummer Boy Cafe is a great example of a converted space done right. With an open space flooded with natural light, and a very teal colour scheme going on, it's a relaxing place to get intimate with a double espresso and the daily news. There's something charming about waiting for your brekky among a cluster of block-mounted prints, ceramic skulls, succulents and other trinkets. Apart from the exceptional coffee, Drummer Boy offers cheery breakfasts, as well as quick and easy croissants and brioche to take away, making this the perfect spot to kick off a morning in the port area. Upon departing, enjoy a well-caffeinated walk around the other Vincent Street locales, like Honeybee Cycles and the Cats in the Loft gallery.

ADELAIDE HILLƧ

Rolling green hills plotted with grape vines, red gums on the horizon and quaint little townships where hipster beard-balm producers can live next door to hard-skinned tractor-driving grape growers. On a weekend cruise through these areas with a silk scarf flapping in the wind, you'll really be able to see what those German settlers 200 years ago fell in love with.

The Adelaide hills cover a large area, but if you travel along the freeway it won't take you too long to get from place to place. You'll start to approach some of the destinations on the fringe of the hills, like Stirling and Crafers, in less than 15 minutes of travelling along the M1 Highway.

Although it's hard to explore it all in a day, I've listed a few places that are well worth the appointment; note that fitting all these in one day would only be possible with access to a car. Picking a few towns of interest may be a better option if you're relying on the good people at Adelaide Metro. There are buses that travel directly to some key areas from the heart of the CBD.

Not everything is located just off the freeway. If you're willing to travel a little further out and have an interest in cars, the National Motor Museum in Birdwood has quite the collection, with a wide range of cars and motorcycles, including a rare Holden and steam-powered motorbike. You'll even get the chance to see the original beast mobile from *Mad Max*! Also worth a side-trip is the Hans Heysen Museum, known as The Cedars, near Hahndorf. A must for art lovers, it offers tours of the house of one of Australia's famous colonial artists, and features Heysen's Model A Ford car and the caravan he used during painting trips.

→ *Panoramic view from Mount Lofty*

PRANCING PONY

42 Mt Barker Rd, Totness
8398 3881
www.prancingponybrewery.
com.au
Open Mon–Wed 10am–6pm,
Thurs 10am–8pm, Fri–Sat
10am–10pm, Sun 10am–8pm

The Prancing Pony brewery
commenced production just
over two years ago in Mount
Barker, the largest township
in the Adelaide Hills. Success
has come rapidly since. Head
brewer Frank and his crew
aren't just any old bunch
that decided to jump on the
craft-beer bandwagon. In fact,
the walls are lined with awards
and certificates commending
their style and quality, a few of
which put them right up there
on the global map, including
their India Red Ale picking up
gold at London's IBC awards
for Best Ale. The brewery is
in operation during the week,
so if you're interested in
catching some of the action
that's the time to head in.
They offer tours for groups of
eight people or more. Book in
advance for a more insightful
and intimate experience. You
can buy a plank (tasting set)
or two and try the range. Food
is available in typical pub fare
and grazing boards.

HAHNDORF

This is the stuff fairy tales are made of – high-peaked German houses with flower pots sitting on the windowsills and Bavarian flags flapping in the wind. However, the backdrop is not of snow-capped alps and dirndl-clad girls, it's eucalyptus and corrugated-iron fences. Without fail, a stop at the **Beerenberg** condiment shop is necessary. Purchase one of the many homemade preserves, marinades and sauces that have become the cornerstone of every good Australian pantry. Seasonally you can even pick your own strawberries at Beerenberg too. Although a punnet of strawberries on its own isn't quite a picnic, Udder Delights cheeses, Harris smoked fish, a loaf of pumpernickel from the bakery and a bottle of riesling from the **Rockbare** cellar should seal the deal.

ADELAIDE HILLS

WINERIES

You probably want to try some wine while you're in the area! Wineries are dotted here and there throughout the entire Adelaide Hills region. Many offer both casual and structured tasting experiences, so sometimes it can pay to just step in for a browse if you are wandering by.

If you're happy to head a little bit further out, a glass of **Shaw & Smith** shiraz or **Bird in Hand** sparkling wine on either of their stunning properties (in Balhannah and Woodside, respectively) will suffice. For the more avant-garde wine experience, **Summertown Aristologist** in Summertown is a lovely little spot boasting wines of the more interesting and experimental nature. The bar/cellar is worth a look if you are looking to take something away. Bottles come by full or half, which is always nice if you need to drive.

Every January the wines of the region are celebrated during the Crush Festival. What's better than a glass of earthy red? A glass of earthy red with live music, theatre and visual art.

MOUNT LOFTY

Traditionally, and in the spirit of health and fitness, you should probably walk to the peak of Mount Lofty. But if you've been eating soft cheese and guzzling riesling all day this might not be your idea of a good time. Fortunately, there's a summit track you can drive all the way to the top, where you can then park and walk out over the observation deck relatively hassle free. There are trusty little signs to help you understand what you're looking at.

Sitting at 727 metres, the summit is the highest point in the Mount Lofty Ranges (and higher than anything in Adelaide). It offers unbeatable panoramic views of the entire city and the neighbouring Piccadilly Valley to the east.

If you're an avid cyclist, the Eagle on The Hill (Old Freeway) ride is a renowned 9-kilometre incline route (not for the faint of heart) all the way to the top.

CLELAND WILDLIFE PARK

365 Mount Lofty Summit Rd, Crafers
8339 2444
www.clelandwildlifepark.
sa.gov.au
Open Mon–Sun 9.30am–5pm

Although Cleland is only 20 minutes southeast of the city, for many it becomes a full day trip. If you don't plan on packing a barbecue or picnic and ticking off every species on your bucket list, it could easily be coupled with visiting other parts of the Adelaide Hills.

On any Australian trip, it becomes basically a rite of passage to pat something furry and hold something scaly. Here is your chance to do that (with the permission and supervision of the park officers, of course!). The conservation park is home to over 5000 different species, all of them as Australian as Vegemite and lamingtons. Spot kangaroos, wallabies, wombats, emus and echidnas in their natural environments; with wetlands, aviaries and even a dingo den, no corner of the animal kingdom will be unseen.

Walk through the reptile centre and see the king brown snake in its natural environment but behind glass. At certain scheduled times, you will have the chance to hold one of the less deadly of the slithery variety in the reptile centre. You'll also have the option of getting friendly with something a little less creepy. That's right – you'll get to meet a koala close up.

Open from 9.30am to 5pm every day, the park gives you plenty of hours to see all you need. Tickets cost $25 for adults and $20 for children, while group tickets, guided tours and more specific experiences come with additional fees. See the website for more details.

BAROSSA VALLEY

This region is a must for all of you gourmet travellers, your chance to sample a special array of Australian ingredients in a beautiful environment.

A one-hour drive north of Adelaide, the Barossa Valley is a stunning area filled with quaint historic townships, settled by German and British folk in the 1800s. Tanunda, Angaston and Nuriootpa are up there among the most notable towns in the region to visit, but there are hidden gems to be found in even the tiniest villages that sit in between, so be sure not to just stick to the main road.

Home to some of the oldest and most established vineyards in the country, this region and the neighbouring Eden Valley will give you an insight into what makes Australian wine truly special and unique – what took us from 'chunder wonder' to 'world class'. Along the way the region is dotted with food, produce and country-town eateries, certain to keep you well fed and happy for the trip ahead.

A car (as usual) can be the best option when it comes to getting there and crafting your own special journey. Alternatively, there is a range of tours available – check out the great bunch of people at Groovy Grape, who run tours several times a week. If you have a larger group, hiring a minibus (that comes with sober driver) is a great way to keep everyone happy, tipsy and carefree about the trip back home; Des's Minibus service is recommended.

↤ *Palm trees lining Seppeltsfield Road*

BAROSSA VALLEY

WINE & BEER

Bold and complex shiraz, well-balanced blends, lavish chardonnays and some of the most elegant dry rieslings ever to hit your palate – the Barossa Valley is home to over 170 wine producers, and the birthplace of big names that are sold worldwide – think Wolf Blass, Yalumba, Jacob's Creek and Seppeltsfield. Here you'll get the chance to explore historic grounds and taste some premium samples from their home base.

Seppeltsfield is considered the oldest winery in the area. They occasionally offer tastings of their famous Para port, which dates back over 90 years. For something a little different, the fortified wine and canape tasting is really special.

It's important to look into a few of the locally loved smaller players too. **Turkey Flat**, **Rockford** and **First Drop** are just a few good smaller-scale operations.

With the boom in craft beer and spirits, you'd only expect the region to be keeping on top of it too! You can head to the restaurant and front bar at **Barossa Valley Brewing** and try a paddle of the full gang. I highly recommend the Chocolate Stout or Smoked Bacon IPA if you're only popping in for a lonesome pint.

PRODUCE & DINING

You can break your day trip up with a huge range of foodie options. A good way to curate this is by following the Butcher, Baker and Winemaker trail (at www.barossa.com, or pick up a brochure from the visitor centre in Tanunda or Kapunda). You can take it in the form of VIP tasting experience, which comes with a picnic hamper priced at $75.

For prime snacking, **Barossa Valley Cheese Company**, **Apex Bakery** and **Maggie Beer's Farm Shop** are ideal locations to snack on samples and pick up some goods to take home. Maggie Beer's Farm Shop in Nuriootpa offers a picnic-based menu perfect for trying her delicious collection of paté, dukkah tarts and pastries. There's a range of weekly cooking demonstrations.

Although many of the wineries in the area offer full-flavoured lunch and dinner options, **Hentley Farm** is exceptionally notable. It's fairly pricey, but it's one of the most highly regarded tasting experiences in the country. There are two options: the Daily Surprise (Du Jour menu) is available for lunch and takes approximately one hour to get through, while the Discovery menu is available for dinner and takes about three hours to be served.

MCLAREN VALE

McLaren Vale is the less commercial, more relaxed option of Australia's premier wine districts. Although it's home to some of the oldest vines in Australia and prestige is not in short supply, most wineries around here are very low key, allowing you to simply show up. They'll likely even let you have a tasting or two for free.

If you've had the experience of wine tasting in the likes of Napa Valley or Bordeaux, and found it's both costly and complicated, you'll be pleasantly surprised to find it's done differently here. With approximately 80 cellar doors and 160 vineyards, your options aren't exactly limited. From the big boys like Hardy's and Wirra Wirra to the more specialised Mollydooker and Primo Estate, you'll find something that suits you. There's one from either end of the experimental-traditional spectrum in this chapter. Wine style is heavily affected by the soil and growing conditions, and there is a huge amount of diversity among the subregions of McLaren Vale, so I would recommend trying a few.

Getting there and around might be an issue for some, but the 752 bus loops through McLaren Vale and McLaren Flat and gets you to a range of locations. It will cost a standard Adelaide Metro fare. For the perfect (wait-free) experience, it's worth finding a ride. Kick things off at the informative visitor centre if you're less familiar with the region. Winery clusters, like Chapel Hill or McMurtrie Road, are a great option if you're limited on time.

Besides being home to some of the world's finest drops, the region has a boutique selection of distilleries, coffee roasters, restaurants and natural sites to hit up.

DAWN PATROL

65 Days Rd, Kangarilla
0412 397 536
www.dawnpatrolcoffee.com.au
Open Sun 9.30am–4pm

The paddock of a property in the middle of Kangarilla is a surprising place for an artisan coffee roaster, but this is where Dawn Patrol performs its magic. You'll need a map to find this place, but trust me, for coffee nerds it's certainly worth heading off-piste to visit.

The logic here is sound: the fresher the better. With this sentiment in mind, Dawn Patrol does its own roasting (most other beans get to SA pre-roasted). It now supplies these ultra-freshly roasted beans to a selected range of key cafes in Adelaide. You'll be able to purchase a fresh grind or whole beans directly from the roastery.

Sit around in a back shed or out in the homestead paddock among the gum trees and try one of the coffees with many different origins, styles and ever-changing roasts. Nothing highlights the differences in coffee strains like trying them side by side, prepared in a laboratory-like fashion. The tattoo-covered beardy gentlemen here will go to almost any lengths to make sure you get the sensory experience done right.

ALPHA BOX & DICE

8 Olivers Rd, McLaren Vale
8323 7750
www.alphaboxdice.com
Open Mon–Fri 11am–5pm,
Sat–Sun 10am–6pm

This winery offers literally the A-Z of wines (every release covers a different letter of the alphabet), focusing particularly on the avant-garde and experimental side of winemaking. Be sure to keep an eye out for the vibrantly eclectic labels produced by a range of renowned designers.

The setting is perfect: bohemian antique store meets outback shearing shed. Sit inside among the velvet couches, old tea boxes and mismatched hanging pictures, or out on the patio in the sun among the vines, enjoying one of the available cheese plates.

Alpha Box has seen huge success with wines like the Tarot Grenache and the Siren Nero D'Avola, but I'd suggest also trying some of the other styles; the unoaked Chard, the skin-contact Viognier and the Dolcetto are all excellent choices.

If wine tasting seems like a daunting process, don't worry, the helpful staff will always happily talk you through the flight.

MCLAREN VALE

SAMUEL'S GORGE

193 Chaffeys Rd, McLaren Vale
8323 8651
www.gorge.com.au
Open Mon–Sun 11am–5pm

Look out over the stunning Onkaparinga Gorge as you enjoy a world-class wine, admiring what is potentially the best view from a winery, and perhaps in the entire region.

Samuel's Gorge winery utilises the iconic traits of the region and focuses specifically on grenache, shiraz, mourvèdre and tempranillo. Participating in a tasting flight here will leave you with a quintessential McLaren Vale and Australian wine experience.

The cellar door is charming and rustic, filled with timeworn winemaking tools in what is perhaps a nod to the winery's traditional basket-press crushing technique.

I don't mean to sound crass, but you might even get the chance to use a traditional Aussie outhouse when visiting. I'll let you learn for yourself what that is.

PIZZATECA

319 Chalk Hill Rd, McLaren Vale
8323 9762
www.pizza-teca.com
Open Fri–Sat 12.30–9.30pm
Sun 12.30–4pm

When I set out for this country pizzeria, I don't think I quite realised what I was getting myself into. I drove off the main McLaren Flat track and through a few windy roads only to arrive at a huge, white, colonial-looking homestead filled with crowds of people flowing from inside out onto the massive grassy area. I lost count of the Panama hat–wearing folk dressed head to toe in RM Williams and Country Road as it quickly became clear that this is the perfect spot for groups and families to come and sit to break up the day.

The staff here are passionate about what they do. The wood-oven pizza production line runs right in front of you, if you get the right seat, so you can take in the entire process while enjoying an Aperol spritz, local wine or can of Italian Castello beer. The pizzas are traditional in style, but Pizzateca has certainly made them their own by using locally sourced ingredients. If you're looking for something to accompany your pizza, the arrosticini skewers and antipasto plates are a must.

PORT WILLUNGA & SELLICKS

Port Willunga, known as one of the most beautiful and loved beaches in Australia, is renowned for the *Star of Greece* shipwreck of 1888. The spot where wooden pillars still remain from the historic jetty is among the most Instagrammed sites in the state. Spend some time walking the historic coastline here and take some photos of the breathtaking sunset.

Willunga, a deceptively far distance from Port Willunga (don't try to walk it) has a whimsical little street that on Saturday morning hosts a great farmers' market, where local farmers, foragers and producers give you the perfect opportunity to taste exactly what the regions are all about.

Not much further along this coastline, you'll come across downtown Aldinga, known by some as the hippy area of South Australia (not be confused with Maslin, the nudist beach only several kilometres away). There is a thriving eco village and an environmentally conscious community. The area has recently seen development, with the emergence of new hip businesses and a spread of renowned Adelaide flagship stores setting up seaside locations. During the summer months, Fridays After Five takes over the main street of Aldinga, bringing it to life with live music, food stalls and wine bars. Shop fronts keep their doors open until late at night and the locals get rowdy.

121

POCKET TIP
An (incomplete) 18-metre granite statue of the Buddha majestically stares out over the ocean at Sellicks Hill. It's the first stage of a $15-million Buddhist retreat project that will be built over the next seven years. When it's done, this Buddha statue will be the largest of its kind in the Southern Hemisphere.

HOME GRAIN BAKERY

13 Old Coach Rd, Aldinga
8557 8231
www.homegrainbakery.com.au
Open Mon–Sun 6.30am–5pm

Around midday is the perfect time to stop into downtown Aldinga. By this time of day I've always got pie on my mind, and there isn't much better than the Wakefield Grange Chunky Steak Pie from Home Grain Bakery, which is a well-tweaked recipe. I'd follow it with the vanilla slice made from Fleurieu Milk cream. There's a range of freshly baked loaves, buns, scrolls and croissants, that will easily (potentially) survive the trip back home for later.

Home Grain owners Toff and Tara have been key characters in the transformation of this area, now owning bakeries in five key SA locations, so you know they're doing something right. The vegetables are cut daily, and on Wednesdays they even supply extra goodies for the vegan folks for Vegan Vednesday.

MISS GLADYS ON SEA

206 Port Rd, Aldinga
www.missgladyssymchoon.
com.au
Open Mon–Sun 10am–5pm

In 1928, Gladys, 16 years old at that time, was the first female business operator to open a store in Australia. Her emporium, Miss Gladys Sym Choon, has been loved by Adelaide's East End ever since. The recently opened Aldinga location is no exception. Owners Joff and Razak curate a fantastic range of women's and men's clothing. The seaside location lends itself well to the collection of eclectic fashion, footwear and accessories. Without the rush of busy Rundle Street, this is a relaxed environment where you can browse, be styled and enjoy the range.

Forgot your bathing suit? You aren't getting out of it that easily! Miss Gladys also stocks a great range of swimwear you can basically wear straight out of the shop!

PORT WILLUNGA & SELLICKS

BATTLE OF BOSWORTH

Gaffney Rd, Willunga
8556 2441
www.battleofbosworth.com.au
Open Mon–Sun 11am–5pm

Set on a simply stunning landscape, with the cutest wine dog around, Battle of Bosworth wines are all certified organic and grown on site (to make sure this is the case).

Although some wines, such as the puritan shiraz, aren't everyone's cup of tea (as is often the case with organic wine), I'm personally partial to their sauvignon blancs in both the flagship and Spring Seed ranges they have on offer. I'm also a huge fan of the Touriga with well-rounded soft tannins for a style not so common to the region.

I'd recommend grabbing a glass and having a wander around the establishment and taking in the old ruins and scenery.

If you're looking to stick to the High Street, the crafty boutique cellar door at Hither and Yon is a fantastic alternative – heck, if you're as keen on this viscous fluid as I am, you'll probably indulge in both.

124

VICTORY HOTEL

Main South Rd, Sellicks Hill
8556 3083
www.victoryhotel.com.au
Open Mon–Sun 10am–12am

Gaze out on the balcony over the ocean while enjoying the sunset and enjoy classic Aussie pub seafood and grain-fed beef. The King George whiting fillets or salt and pepper squid are also house favourites. But seriously, if you're always on the prowl for that perfect cut of beef, you'll find choice cuts from across the state served with some phenomenal trimmings

Wash it down with a pint of Swell or Vale ale. Due to the incredible seaside view and quality food, this place is usually booked in the restaurant area, so be sure to call ahead to secure a table. If you consider yourself a bit of an eight-baller, why not stick around for a match or two of pool; watch out for the local table sharks.

FIELD TRIP

VICTOR HARBOR

Located approximately 80 kilometres from Adelaide, less than an hours' drive from the city, you'll find the sleepy seaside town of Victor Harbor.

Sitting on the rugged coastline of the Fleurieu Peninsula, Victor Harbor overlooks the impressive seascape of Encounter Bay, named for the spot where French and British explorers startled each other while navigating the area. Ironically, encounters among British and French backpackers here are fairly commonplace today. The perfect place for backpackers to get out of town and by far one of the best hostels I have ever stayed in, Port Elliot Beach House YHA, is located just a short drive away. Although it's not all ruck sacks and bunk beds – Victor Harbor is the perfect getaway for all walks of life. The area is bejewelled with local produce, stunning vista points and a quaint set of eateries and accommodation providers.

It's highly advisable to avoid this area during late November as schoolies (think spring break with Australian accents) take over the town.

→ *Overlooking the peninsula from Granite Island*

VICTOR HARBOR

GETTING BACK TO NATURE

Victor Harbor has been a holiday destination in this part of the world for generations. With a great collection of adventure trails, heritage walks, and wildlife watching, it's the ideal place to unwind in nature. Walk the iconic bridge to the mighty Granite Island, aptly named for its huge granite boulders. If the walk seems a bit much, you could always take the historic horse-drawn cart over.

Into wildlife spotting? Here's your chance to get a good look at penguins, wallabies, and other cuddly creatures in their natural environment. For a more guaranteed wildlife experience, **Umbria Wildlife Park** would be your best bet – it's home to over 70 species of Australian animals and open daily for self-guided tours.

Eco-tours can be an excellent way to get into the great outdoors, so be sure to head into the visitor centre to see what's on offer.

Surf schools, diving experiences and kayak rental are offered by a range of providers. Prices and seasonal activities vary, so do some research online before heading down. There's a brilliant skate park by the sea, so if this is your jam, don't forget to bring your deck.

HUNTING & GATHERING

With the region's major exports being agriculture and fisheries there's no shortage of chances for you to try some freshly caught garfish or squid, or maybe even reel in that huge fish to exaggerate about at one of the many quaint local pubs. Once again, checking into the visitor centre upon arrival will give you a good chance to get a grip on all the options for charters, ramp fees and local regulations.

Goolwa makes a good short trip – this neighbouring township is only a few kilometres away and offers breweries and farms producing cheese and wine. You can even catch the **Cockle Train** between Goolwa and Victor Harbor.

KANGAROO ISLAND

This island was actually discovered before Adelaide, and it's surprising that so few people stuck around. There must have been more kangaroos that lived here back then, as these days it's harder to see how the island got its name.

If you're in the market for a packed couple of days of diverse experiences, this is your spot. After taking a short ferry ride from Cape Jervis, there is a range of accommodation options available on the island. I would recommend staying at either of the two largest townships, Kingscote or Penneshaw, particularly if you plan on using the Sealink guided tours and don't have a car.

The island is large so plan your itinerary wisely, or you'll spend your weekend sitting behind the wheel of a car (likely without any radio reception, so convert those playlists to offline!).

→ *View from the deck of the Sealink Ferry ride*

KANGAROO ISLAND

ANIMALS & OTHER ADVENTURES

For animal lovers, you've got eagles, owls, and other large birds at the **Raptor Domain** – if you're game, you'll even get the chance to be perched on by a wedge-tailed eagle!

Seal spotting at – you guessed it – the **Seal Bay Conservation Park** is a nice way to spend an afternoon. Wander the self-guided boardwalk or get more informed expert insight on the Australian sea-lion hourly on one of the organised tours.

Seasonally there's a chance to find penguins, go whale watching and see a range of other native fuzzy friends including koalas, wallabies and even goannas.

For thrill seekers, there's sand boarding at **Little Sahara** or kite surfing with **Seabreeze**. You might like to explore the aptly named Remarkable Rocks at **Flinders Chase National Park**. The enormous, naturally formed granite boulders make the perfect location to sit and watch the sun go down over the sea.

FOOD & DRINK

Kangaroo Islands has world-famous honey available from several local producers, and around here honey isn't just for tasting – **Ligurian Honey** hand and body products are becoming quite the trend.

If you're partial to dairy, **KI Pure** is here to convince you sheep cheese is the way to go – the halloumi, feta and other styles are something wondrous. Book in advance for daily tours and tastings.

Local shellfish come from some of the freshest and most unpolluted environments on the planet; you'll taste the difference if you pop into the **Kangaroo Island Oyster Farm** shop and enjoy a dozen plucked and shucked straight from the water.

For those looking to continue the adventure that they started in Adelaide, Jon Lark's **Kangaroo Island Spirits** (KIS) distillery is the home of several noteworthy spirits. Head on into the tin shed and work your way through the ever-growing list of premium hand-made liqueurs and gins on offer.

Not far down the dusty track is the similarly named **Kangaroo Island Brewery**, where tasting trays are poured. On special occasions, they bring in local chefs and musicians to bring the scene to life.

GETTING TO ADELAIDE

Flying to Adelaide

Although Adelaide has an international airport, and several carriers (particularly in Asia) offer direct flights, many flights still arrive via the east coast capitals, so be sure to ensure your luggage is checked all the way through.

Domestic budget carrier flights can be as low as $70 return from the east coast, services such as Google Flights and Skyscanner are perfect for finding comparisons. Flexibility is key, and midweek flights can be the more reasonable option.

If you plan on heading over for a few days be aware that budget flights often charge extra for checked-in luggage, and check the requirements before you board.

Adelaide Airport

1 James Schofield Drive, off Sir Donald Bradman Drive

8308 9211

Code: ADL

www.adelaideairport.com.au

Getting to/from the airport

Adelaide airport is a short taxi or Uber from the CBD (approximately $15-$20), while Adelaide metro connects to the CBD and also Glenelg (by far the cheapest option). The airport offers a shuttle service to major hotels and city locations for $10.

Driving to Adelaide

Driving to Adelaide from the east coast is often done via the scenic Great Ocean Road. This begins in Torquay, outside of Melbourne, and culminates somewhere around Mount Gambier in South Australia. It's best to spend several days on this route.

For the speedy trip from Melbourne (achievable within eight hours), the inland route via Ballarat and Horsham is the best option.

Driving from Sydney, you are looking at closer to 15 hours along the Sturt Highway. It's best to do this with alternating drivers or over two days.

GETTING AROUND ADELAIDE

Adelaide has a fully functional Uber service 24 hours a day. However during surge and peak times, taxi services might be cheaper.

Car rental

Renting a car gets you more places faster. There is a range of services online that ensure you get the best deal; for example, Skyscanner offers car rental comparisons. When opting for a budget rental agency be sure to review insurance costs.

Public transport

Adelaide's buses, trains and trams run on the Metro Card and Metro Ticket systems. Tickets are available from various locations around Adelaide; head to www.adelaidemetro.com.au/Tickets for more information. The Adelaide Metro Info Centre in the heart of the CBD can be found at 136 North Terrace.

- Public transport routes through Adelaide Metro are offered to most suburban areas, and through some of the regions we have covered as day trips.
- The Adelaide Metro Journey Planner online is perfect for organising trips. Scheduling a route for the day when travelling large distances using Google's MyMaps can be very handy too.
- The tram line is exceptionally convenient and runs to both Glenelg and Thebarton from the CBD.
- Free loop buses are provided around the CBD.

TIME ZONES

Adelaide is in the Australian Central Standard time zone (UTC+09.30).

Time in Adelaide is half an hour behind Melbourne and Sydney.

MEDIA & TOURIST INFORMATION

CityMag.com.au – cultural curation of Adelaide's best places to be

Broadsheet.com.au – catalogue of the best places to eat, drink and play in Adelaide

The Adelaide Review – collection of articles, events and what's on in Adelaide`

Yella Umbrella – great city walking tours

Southaustralia.com – South Australian Tourism

Peterpans Adventure Travel – good choice of travel/tourism agent

Yewth Magazine – an overview of local personalities, events and culture. Targeting a well, youth-full demographic.

CLIMATE

Adelaide often has quite mild winters and usually has very warm, dry summers where it's not unheard-of to see heatwaves of over 35°C for several days in a row.

This enduring dry heat can be dangerous if you don't prepare: maintain your fluid intake, stay out of direct sun as much as possible during the peak hours (11am to 4pm), and wear sunscreen and headwear.

Adelaide has an average maximum temperature of 29°C (84°F) in summer and 15-16°C (59-61°F) in winter.

Although it's exceptionally dry, rain is a possibility throughout all seasons, so bring that raincoat. When driving long distances over the winter season, check to see if campsites and back roads are open.

LGBTQ

Many events and nights for the LGBTQ community occur weekly in a range of different venues and locations. The Mars Bar is Adelaide's renowned gay venue, but many inner-city bars and pubs are gay-friendly. A great resource to learn what's going on is the LGBTQ events website www.adelaidelgbtevents.webs.com or Blaze Magazine, Adelaide's gay and lesbian monthly print publication. Feast, Adelaide's annual queer arts and cultural festival, runs in November.

OPENING HOURS

Retail stores are generally open between 9am and 5pm and some locations operate from 8am to 6pm. Most areas have convenience stores and petrol stations trading 24 hours (or until quite late).

In outer suburbs late-night shopping is held on Thursday and in the central areas it occurs on Friday. In general 'late night' means opening hours are extended to 9pm.

While Sunday trading is becoming more common, a range of retail and entertainment services will be closed, so be sure to check online beforehand.

Although a growing number of places are offering all-day breakfasts, breakfast is usually served between 7am and 11am by cafes and some restaurants. Don't assume all establishments serve breakfast; check in advance.

In general restaurants will serve lunch from 12pm to 2.30pm but some kitchens will stay open through to dinner, particularly in full-service establishments like hotels and pubs. Dinner will be served from 5 or 6pm until 9 or 10pm.

Bars in general shut their doors from between 12am and 2am, however extended trading hours exist for key clubs and hotels around Adelaide. The Skycity casino is often considered as a late-night last resort.

VOLTAGE & CONVERTERS

AS/NZS 3112 plug standards are shared only between Australian and New Zealand. Unlike Europe and the US it's almost always a three-pin socket.

Appliances built for 220-240 volts are suited to these sockets. If you don't know, don't gamble – ignoring this advice may literally blow up in your face.

Converters are available from outdoor stores, department stores and souvenir stores.

EATING & DRINKING IN ADELAIDE

See p. 135 for restaurant and cafe opening hours.

Reservations

Dinner regularly rotates two sittings, the first at 5 or 6pm and the second at 7 or 8pm. Always book ahead if it's an option, particularly in busy locations. Lunch services do not often accept or require bookings.

Late-night food

There is a range of 24-hour bakeries as you head out of the city in every direction including Enjoy Bakery on The Parade, Café de Villi's on South Road, and Bakery on O'Connell in North Adelaide. Rundle Street and Hindley Street offer the classic late-night cuisine of kebabs and pizza. Petrol stations often contain 24-hour fast-food restaurants.

Halal certifications

There is an Australian-wide halal certification; Australian Federation of Islamic Councils (AFIC) and the Australian government awards this to restaurants and producers who fully fit the process criteria.

More and more South Australian products are following halal guidelines, and they will be clearly marked on packaging.

Halal Square is a great website to go to to find listings of halal options in Adelaide, see www.halalsquare.com.au.

Vegetarian and vegan options

Every restaurant generally has at least one vegetarian option these days; it should be marked on the menu. Vegan options are slightly less common but are often available. Happycow.net is a great resource for finding places. Two-Bit Villains and Vego & Love'N It are two great options for vegetarian food.

FESTIVALS

They don't call us the Festival State for nothing (heck it's even on our licence plates). From late January to early April, Adelaide hosts a string of festivals renowned the world over. A few notable ones include the Adelaide Fringe Festival, Adelaide Festival of the Arts, WOMADelaide, South Australian Living Artists (SALA) Festival, Adelaide 500, and Feast Festival.

Ordering coffee

Adelaide uses a mixed coffee system that sits somewhere between the British and the Italian.

- Flat white (coffee with steamed milk), long black (similar to Americano; coffee with hot water) and short black (similar to espresso, often closer to a double shot) are all served in a demitasse.
- Latte (coffee shot, steamed milk, milk foam) is served in a tapered rocks glass.
- Cappuccino (built like a latte, often with chocolate powder or cocoa on top) and macchiato (espresso shot with a dollop of milk foam) are served in a handled mug.

Ordering beer

It is not common to walk into a bar and simply state you want a beer; you want to ask for the size and the style you're interested in, and beer sizes in South Australia are subtly different when compared to other states.

The SA schooner (285ml) is the same size as a pot/middy/half-pint in other states. The SA pint (425ml) is the same size as other states' schooner, and is 0.75 imperial pints.

If you're having trouble interpreting styles, many beer bars will quote IBU (intrinsic bitterness unit the lower the least bitter), and ALC or ABV – the alcohol content.

WIFI

Adelaide CBD is renowned for its inner city free wifi – a map of its coverage can easily be obtained online (cityofadelaide. com.au) Many inner city cafes, bars and accommodation providers offer free wireless networks. However, if you are looking for something more mobile for a group of travellers, Pocket Wifi and wireless USB packs are available from most major providers.

PUBLIC HOLIDAYS

Public Holiday opening hours change from store to store, and most stores will publicise these hours on their facebook or website. The major public holidays are Easter and Christmas, so it's worth checking opening hours over those holiday periods.

PHONES

For international visitors wanting to use their mobile phones, prepaid SIM cards are an easy and flexible way to get connected – you can access data, write texts and conduct local and international calls, and recharge the amount of money on your plan. There is no contract, but you will require an existing handset and several forms of identification. Australia has several different telecommunications companies that offer prepaid SIM cards, all you need to do is pick up a SIM and then choose the initial value you require ($20, $40, $50, etc.).

Australia's international dialing code is +61 (0061). If calling a landline to South Australia from interstate or overseas please include the regional dialing code (08). Please note that the 0 is removed from the phone number and prefix if used in conjunction with an additional code. An example of an overseas call to a landline would be +61 8 8390 4967 and an example of an overseas call to cellular would be +61 402 785 843.

MONEY

ATMs can be found throughout all of the primary commercial districts, inside bank branches and regularly in full-service hotels and pubs. Be cautious of ATM fees, particularly those inside of private venues. It's a good practice to speak to your bank before your departure, let them know you will be travelling and request an account with lower international withdrawal fees.

As a general rule, most vendors accept card payments, including taxis and parking stations. If attending events, festivals, fairs or outer metro locations, having cash on hand is always a good idea.

Australia uses the contactless card system known as Paywave or PayPass, or as bartenders like to say 'Can I tappit' mate?'. If your card has an RFID chip this option should be available to you.

TIPPING

Although tipping is not a requirement in Australia some people tip at upmarket restaurants and bars, particularly after high-quality service. You may also see tip jars on counters, often used to discard small change.

LANGUAGE

Australians love a bit of slang, so here are some common phrases you might hear:

Avo – avocado

Arvo – afternoon

Barbie – barbecue

Bottle-o – liquor store

Brekkie – breakfast

Bucks – dollars

Call it a day – finish what you're doing

Chuck – to throw

Cheers – thank you, also said when clinking glasses

Cuppa – a hot beverage

Chemist – drug store/pharmacy

Dodgy – poor quality/not reliable/suspicious

EFTPOS – machine for electronic (card) payments, stands for Electronic Funds Transfer at Point Of Sale

Esky – portable ice cooler

Fair go – a fair chance

Flat White – coffee with milk or cream

Goon – cheap wine in a bag

Grog run – a trip to go and buy alcohol

Heaps – a lot or very

How good is that? – a rhetorical question, it just means 'that's good'

How ya going/How's it going? – How are you?

Lift – elevator

Mobile/Mobes – cell phone

No worries – don't worry about it/it's OK

Petrol – gas

Pokies – slot machines

Reach out – get into contact with

Reckon – think, i.e. 'what do you reckon?'

Servo – service station/gas station

She'll be right – it will be fine

Shout – a round of drinks paid for by a particular person, i.e. 'it's my shout'

Scull – to drink something quickly in one go

Snag – sausage

Stubbie – a bottle of beer

Veggies – vegetables

INDEX

ABOUT THE AUTHOR

Sam's been an avid traveller since his youth and has spent several long stints living outside of Australia.

He started his guidebook journey as the director and co-founder of the student-focused Insider Guides, covering a range of Australian and British regions. He's worked with publications, agencies, banks, councils and universities in both concept development and content creation capacities.

Sam is working on producing an international adventure map series with Hardie Grant covering Tokyo, Melbourne, London, New York City and San Francisco.

There's no part of the process Sam doesn't enjoy: writing, photography, illustration and graphic design. On his off days, however, the warm crackle of crisp vinyl paired with a jammy glass of red keep him entertained.

ACKNOWLEDGEMENTS

I'm an Adelaide local through and through. I've spent time lurking around some of the cosmopolitan greats: Tokyo, San Francisco, New York, London ... but there's nothing quite like seeing the cultural and urban scenes you grew up in flourishing to their full potential. Adelaide's no longer a layover destination, or somewhere you visit your retired relatives. It's an incredible destination everyone should have the chance to visit.

I'm honoured to have explored it and thrilled that Hardie Grant was so eager to acknowledge its successes in guidebook form. Without the cunning planning of Melissa Kayser and Megan Cuthbert, plus of course the pristine editing of Kate James, these pages wouldn't have existed for you to read.

Thanks to Josh, Fuko, James, Brenton and Craig for enduring the embarrassment of having that mate that takes photos of bar staff and writes notes about food in public places.

Published in 2018 by Hardie Grant Travel, a division of Hardie Grant Publishing

Hardie Grant Travel (Melbourne)
Building 1, 658 Church Street
Richmond, Victoria 3121

Hardie Grant Travel (Sydney)
Level 7, 45 Jones Street
Ultimo, NSW 2007

hardiegranttravel.com

Explore Australia is an imprint of Hardie Grant Travel

© Imprint and currency – VAR Product and PSMA Data "Copyright. Based on data provided under licence from PSMA Australia Limited (www.psma.com.au)".

Hydrography Data (May 2006)
Parks & Reserves Data (August 2016)
Transport Data (May 2017)

Assistance with research: The publisher would like to thank the following organisations for assistance with data and information: Transport SA, Primary Industries and Resources South Australia, Department of Environment and Natural Resources, South Australian Tourism Commission.

A Cataloguing-in-Publication entry is available from the catalogue of the National Library of Australia at www.nla.gov.au

Adelaide Pocket Precincts
ISBN 9781741175547

Commissioning editor
Melissa Kayser

Project editor
Megan Cuthbert

Editor
Kate James

Editorial assistant
Aimee Barrett

Cartographers
Bruce McGurty, Emily Maffei

Cartographic research
Claire Johnston

Design and illustrations
Michelle Mackintosh

Typesetting
Megan Ellis

Index
Max McMaster

Prepress
Megan Ellis, Splitting Image Colour Studio

Photography credits
All images are © Sam Tresize, except for the following: Page ii, iv, vi (coffee cup and Proof image), 10, 24, 32, 33, 37, 59, 66, 67, 91 Josie Withers; page 4, 89, 132 Adam Bruzzone; page 9 John Montesi; page 41, 47, 92 Andre Castellucci; page 55 AKA Photography; page 108 and 109 Greg Snell; page 126 G. Scheer; page 132 Daniel R. Westergren

Page i: photograph of artwork by Steve Glass

Printed in China by 1010 Printing International Limited